THE
ARCHERS

Year of Food and Farming

Keri Davies is a radio producer and writer, best known for his work on the BBC radio soap opera *The Archers*. He used to be the show's senior producer and since 2003 has been a scriptwriter. Until 2015, he ran the official website for the show.

THE
ARCHERS

Year of Food and Farming

KERI DAVIES

SEVEN DIALS

First published in Great Britain in 2019 by Seven Dials
an imprint of The Orion Publishing Group Ltd
Carmelite House, 50 Victoria Embankment
London EC4Y 0DZ

An Hachette UK Company

1 3 5 7 9 10 8 6 4 2

Copyright © The Orion Publishing Group Limited 2019
Illustrations on pages i, iii, 1, 21, 23, 45, 67, 89, 113, 137,
159, 179, 201, 221, 241 by Emanuel Santos
All other illustrations: Shutterstock

By arrangement with the

A CIP catalogue record for this book is
available from the British Library.

ISBN (Hardback) 978 1 4746 0768 1
ISBN (eBook) 978 1 4746 0769 8

Printed in Great Britain by Clays Ltd, Elcograf, S.p.A.

MIX
Paper from
responsible sources
FSC® C104740

www.orionbooks.co.uk

To the one who danced.

CONTENTS

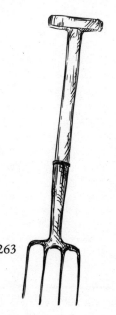

INTRODUCTION

Running under, over and through all the stories of *The Archers*, as mood music to the lives of all our characters, are two essentials – food and farming.

Think of Jill Archer and you envisage her in the Brookfield kitchen, baking. When the Aldridges had to leave Home Farm, one of the things that upset Jennifer was that she was going to have to leave behind her precious range. Think of the Grundys and you think of cider, the first thing you know about Neil Carter is that he is a brilliant pigman (and the second thing that springs to mind is chilli con carne), of Helen and you think of Borsetshire Blue (now that's a mouthful – you try saying it).

At the heart of the story of Ambridge are Brookfield, Home Farm, Bridge Farm and Grange Farm. Food, farming and the progress of the seasons – whether it be the Flower and Produce show, Deck the Hall at Lower Loxley, or lambing with Pip, Ruth, David and co – are what help define *The Archers*.

We are delighted to have the opportunity to explore a year of food and farming in more detail in this book. We give you the lowdown on Jill's baking secrets, share the art of Grundy cider pressing, tuck into a hearty and very special breakfast at Lower Loxley, and enjoy the Single Wicket (but enjoy Fallon's post-match tea and cakes even more).

We hope you are entertained by this glimpse into the life of Ambridge today, one of England's most visited and celebrated villages. It's a place rooted in an eventful past and – who knows – with an exciting future, but rest assured, that whatever happens the sun will rise every day over Lakey Hill and there will always be cows to milk.

Jeremy Howe
Editor, *The Archers*

CHAPTER ONE

September

No, you haven't opened the book at the wrong page –
and the publisher has assembled it in the correct order.
A teacher will tell you that the year starts in September.
And so will a farmer, so that is where we are starting our
Archers year.

But for many Ambridge worthies, September also
means a culmination. Armed with weighing scale and
preserving funnel, trug and trowel, they are preparing to
do battle in the annual Flower and Produce Show. Two
rivals are gearing up for this gladiatorial contest. It started
with an unthinking remark from Fallon Rogers, during
a busy Sunday in her Ambridge Tearoom. Apparently
unaware that the 1950s ended some time ago, Jennifer
Aldridge had treated her stepson Ruairi to a slap-up end-
of-the-holidays afternoon tea. A wizard wheeze, Ruairi had
dubbed it, although Jennifer did not quite catch the irony.
In any case, both had been sent into raptures by the scones
and driven quite ecstatic by the Victoria sponge.

VICTORIA SPONGE

Makes 8–10 slices

200g unsalted butter
  (at room temperature),
  plus extra for greasing
200g golden caster sugar
4 eggs
200g self-raising flour

2 tbsp milk or water
4–6 tbsp jam
200g double cream,
  whipped (optional)
icing sugar, for dusting

Preheat the oven to 190°C/Fan 170°C/Gas 5. Grease 2 x 20cm sandwich tins with butter and line the base of each with baking parchment.

Beat the butter and sugar together in a bowl until light and creamy. Add the eggs, one at a time, then fold in the flour with a metal spoon. Add the milk or water to make a soft batter.

Divide the mixture between the prepared tins and smooth the tops. Bake for 20 minutes until the cakes are golden, nicely risen and feel springy when touched. Leave the cakes to cool for about 5 minutes in the tins, then turn them onto a wire rack to cool completely. Remove the baking parchment.

Spread the top of one cake with jam and add the cream, if using, then top with the other cake. Dust with icing sugar to finish.

The sugar rush might have had something to do with it, but Jennifer was effusive in her praise. 'It's just as well you can't enter your cakes in the Flower and Produce Show, Fallon,' she had said, dropping her change into her Moroccan leather purse.

'It leaves the way clear for people like Emma,' Fallon joked as she closed the till, unaware that her employee had suddenly turned as cold and chippy as the mint choc ice cream in their freezer.

'What did you mean by that?' The café was now empty, and Emma was sweeping the floor with unnecessary vigour. 'Are you saying I'm an amateur?'

'Um . . .' They usually rubbed along well, but sometimes Fallon was reminded that Emma was Susan Carter's daughter. Both could take offence in an empty room, if they thought it was casting aspersions on their status.

''Cos I bake as much of the food here as you do.' This was not strictly true, but Fallon knew better than to quibble.

'No, I just meant . . . you have put stuff in the show. Your . . . those Brazilian things.'

BRIGADEIROS
Makes about 16

397g can of condensed milk
30g cocoa powder
pinch of salt
20g butter, plus extra for greasing
chocolate sprinkles, chopped nuts or desiccated coconut,
  for coating

Put the condensed milk, cocoa powder, salt and butter in a
pan. Place over a gentle heat and cook, stirring constantly with
a wooden spoon until the mixture thickens and starts to pull
away from the bottom of the pan. Don't stop stirring or the
mixture will catch on the base of the pan and burn.

Grease a plate with butter, then pour the mixture onto the
plate and leave it to cool. Shape the mixture into small balls
with your hands – you'll find this easier if you grease your
hands with a little butter first – then roll the balls in the
coating of your choice. Store in the fridge.

Fallon blundered on. 'It just wouldn't seem right for me to enter somehow. I've been a judge.'

'If you did, I'd give you a good run for your money.'

'I'm sure you would, but I can't, can I?'

Emma's eyes narrowed. 'Not with a cake, maybe.'

And so the battle lines were drawn and the weapons selected. Cakes were clearly off limits. But the chutney that the tearoom serves with its Ploughman's Platefuls comes from a small supplier in St John's Parva. So there could be no accusations of professionalism in that category.

September can be a glorious time of year, as we cling on a little longer to the warmth of summer. Assuming we have had a traditional sunny summer, of course. Sometimes a warm September can act as a consolation for that washed-out camping holiday in watery July. But whatever the weather brings, on the four working farms of Ambridge this is the time for preparation and planting. For the vegetable gardener, spring is the peak sowing season. But cereal crops can be sown now, while the soil is still warm, giving the delicate seedlings a chance to establish themselves and break through, before the chill of winter slows everything to dormancy.

On a misty early morning, a lone figure armed with a spade strides into a field of stubble. Adam Macy digs a small hole and then delves into it, crumbling the soil between his fingers. He is checking how it is recovering since

he banished the plough from Home Farm and adopted
no-tillage. Usually shortened to 'no-till', this method of
cultivation causes only minimal disturbance to the soil.
Adam is pleased to see several earthworms, which break
down dead plant matter and mix it into the soil. They also
create space underground for oxygen and water. But he
is most fascinated by the life he can't see. Microbes and
fungi help unlock nutrients so that plants can use them.
They can even protect against disease by releasing natural
antibiotics.

Adam is happy that he's not driving ploughshares
through this complex web. He had a tough time persuad-
ing his stepfather Brian Aldridge to invest in the no-till drill
– the machine was an expensive beast. It cuts a shallow
groove in the soil as the tractor drives along. The seeds
drop into the groove, and the drill pushes loose soil over
to cover them. The stubble from the previous crop is left
behind – more food for the earthworms.

Adam's decisions have a big impact on the Ambridge
farming scene. As well as running the 1,500-acre Home
Farm, he usually has the contract to farm the arable
(crop-growing) land of the Berrow Estate, the best part
of another 1,000 acres. He also handles the much smaller
task of Brookfield Farm's arable. He is going to drill this
field with winter wheat, his principal crop. But wheat is
'hungry', so he has to rotate his crops, for their health
and the soil's – and with an eye on what is fetching a good
price. Winter wheat is often followed by barley sown in the
spring. This is cheaper to grow because it needs looking

after with fungicide and fertiliser for a shorter time. Adam may choose oilseed rape or winter beans after that, both of which leave the soil with plenty of nitrogen, ready for the wheat to use. He is also keen on planting short-term crops over the winter: a fodder crop for the sheep or a 'cover crop', such as mustard, to protect the soil. Sometimes he will slot his beloved herbal leys into the rotation – but more of them later.

Behind the Scenes
In the years after the Second World War, Britain was struggling to feed itself and was still subject to food rationing. So *The Archers* was originally conceived as a way of educating farmers in modern production methods. But because of the quality of the storytelling, the programme quickly became hugely popular with the whole country. *The Archers* lost its educational remit in 1972, but still aims to portray an accurate picture of farming and village life.

As we trace the River Am south, its tributary Heydon Brook leads us to Bridge Farm. Tom and Helen Archer carry the torch that their parents Pat and Tony lit in 1984. As organic farmers, they champion an alternative to the industrialised system that has dominated agriculture since the Second World War. They reject chemical fertilisers, herbicides and pesticides. So, although their yields are lower and costs are higher, they can point to far greater soil quality, and to huge benefits for wildlife. The Bridge Farm Archers are long-established members of the Soil Association, the certification body and campaigning organisation. The SA claims that plant, insect and birdlife is fifty per cent more abundant on organic farms which on average are home to thirty per cent more species.

As we stroll onto Bridge Farm land, we are quite likely to see a robin pulling at a worm. The robin is a year-round resident. But if we lift our eyes to the power lines paralleling the Felpersham road, we may see house martins with their rich blue-black colouring; or swallows, lighter in colour, with their distinctive tuning-fork tail. Sitting like pegs on a washing line, they are gathering ready for the migration to Africa. Both species feed mainly on insects snatched on the wing. Tom asserts that these critters are much more plentiful over his land than over Home Farm's large monocultural fields. Adam counters with the need for affordable food for an ever-growing world population.

Bridge Farm grows winter wheat too, but with some key differences. At the back end of August, the field we now stand in was full of clover, which Tom ploughed into the soil. Clover makes free fertiliser from fresh air, working with soil bacteria to 'fix' nitrogen from the atmosphere. This essential element is then available for the next crop. By harnessing clover in this way, Bridge Farm has no need for synthetic fertilisers based on fossil fuels, which release the greenhouse gas nitrous oxide. And Pat and Tony have not had a fertiliser bill to pay since they converted to organic.

Towards the end of this month, the surrounding trees gradually modulate their variations on a theme of green into the joyous, fiery jazz of autumn. In their lengthening shadows, Tom will scratch out the weeds with a simple piece of kit called a comb harrow, and then drill his wheat seeds the old-fashioned way.

Most of that is a one-person, one-tractor job. The potato harvest, which also happens this month, is much more labour-intensive. Although the spuds are earthed up by a tractor-towed device, they still have to be picked up by hand. Bridge Farm used to have a regular gang of casuals, who relieved their back-bent work with a raucous commentary. Their unofficial leader was the shameless Beryl, whose bawdy comments would make a stevedore blush. Most of that crew are retired now, but in 2018 Beryl's grandson kept the family tradition going – for potato picking, if not for ribaldry. Potatoes are a staple of Bridge Farm's veg boxes, so this important crop will be stored and eked out through the coming months.

◇◇◇◇◇◇◇◇◇◇◇◇◇◇◇◇◇◇◇◇◇◇◇◇◇◇◇◇◇◇◇◇◇◇

Ambridge International

ARGENTINA

◇◇◇◇◇◇◇◇◇◇◇◇◇◇◇◇◇◇◇◇◇◇◇◇◇◇◇◇◇◇◇◇◇◇

Rex and Toby Fairbrother arrived in Ambridge in 2015, planning to break into farming by raising geese. But Toby always thinks big; rather too big, many would say. He was soon pitching a 'share farming' proposal to Adam Macy in which he and Rex would run beef cattle on Home Farm land. Toby claimed that his brother had spent his gap year working on a ranch in Argentina, and ended up nearly running the place. This was news to Rex, who had in fact spent just a fortnight there.

There are two more definite connections between Ambridge and the land of pampas and tango. Retired wine importer Carol Tregorran had business connections in Mendoza. And raffish Nelson Gabriel died there in 2001, having fled his creditors two years earlier. Attendees at his funeral in Ambridge included two men in camel coats, an array of policemen and a beautiful weeping Argentinian woman.

ARGENTINIAN EMPANADAS
Makes 10–12

Filling
1 tbsp olive oil, plus extra for brushing
1 red onion, peeled and finely chopped
2 garlic cloves, peeled and finely chopped
400g minced or finely chopped beef
75g pimento-stuffed olives, finely chopped
zest of ½ lemon
1 tsp dried oregano
2 tbsp finely chopped parsley
50ml white wine
2 hard-boiled eggs, finely chopped
salt and black pepper

Pastry
500g plain flour
1 tsp baking powder
1 tsp sweet smoked paprika
100ml olive oil
100ml white wine
1–2 tbsp ice-cold water

First make the filling. Heat the tablespoon of olive oil in a large frying pan and add the red onion. Sauté until very soft and translucent, then turn up the heat and add the garlic and the beef. Brown the meat quickly, then turn down the heat again and add the olives, lemon zest, oregano, parsley and white wine. Season with plenty of salt and pepper then cook for a few minutes. Leave to cool, then add the chopped eggs.

To make the pastry, put the flour, baking powder, paprika and a little salt in a bowl and stir to combine. Gradually drizzle in the olive oil and wine and cut it in with a knife until you have crumbly clumps. Add the water, a tablespoon at a time, until you can form a dough. Knead the dough for a few minutes until very smooth. Preheat the oven to 200°C/Fan 180°C/Gas 6.

To assemble the empanadas, roll out the dough, either by hand with a rolling pin or with a pasta machine. You will not need to flour your work surface, as the dough will not be sticky. Keep rolling until the dough stops springing back – it will do so to start with as it is very elastic.

Cut 10cm rounds and place a dessertspoonful of the filling on each one. Wet around the edges with water and fold together. The easiest way to do this is to stretch one side over the filling and press it down onto the other side.

Arrange the empanadas over two baking trays and brush them with olive oil. Bake in the oven for 20–25 minutes until puffed up into smooth domes and a rich red brown in colour. Good hot or cold.

SEPTEMBER

At Brookfield, uber-matriarch Jill Archer is slicing potatoes, while on the Aga a pan of vegetable stock (home-made, of course) is starting to bubble.

'Thing is, I've never made chutney in my life.' Fallon is already regretting getting involved.

'It's really not that difficult.'

Fallon observes Jill's potato-slicing technique.

'You don't use a mandoline for that?'

'I'm sorry?'

'Or a food processor?'

'For this little job?' With a bemused smile, Jill swiftly spreads the slices over the vegetables in the blue-edged enamel roaster. Almost wafer-thin, they overlap like fish scales.

'What is it?'

'Something I made years ago for a Harvest Supper. With the show coming up, Bert's being very selective in his garden, so he's given me some of his rejects.'

'It looks delicious.'

'Once I get it in the oven, we'll have a cup of tea and little chutney lesson, shall we?'

LEEK AND POTATO BOULANGÈRE
Serves 4

75g butter, plus extra for greasing
2 tbsp olive oil
4 leeks, washed and thinly sliced
100ml white wine
1kg floury potatoes (Maris Pipers or King Edwards)
2 garlic cloves, peeled and finely sliced (optional)
1 tsp dried sage
500ml vegetable or chicken stock
salt and black pepper

Preheat the oven to 180°C/Fan 160°C/Gas 4. Generously butter a large baking dish. Cut a piece of baking parchment to about the same size.

Heat half the butter and the oil in a large lidded sauté pan. When the butter has melted, add the leeks. Cook over a gentle heat for about 10 minutes, then pour in the wine. Bring to the boil and allow the wine to reduce down to almost nothing. While the leeks are cooking, prepare the potatoes. Wash them while they are still whole and pat them dry. Slice, unpeeled, as thinly as possible, with a mandoline if you dare. Do not wash again as you don't want to lose all the starch.

Arrange a layer of about a quarter of the sliced potatoes in the base of the baking dish. Season with salt and pepper, then follow with a third of the leeks, some garlic, if using, and a little sage. Repeat twice, remembering to season each time, then finish with a final layer of potatoes.

Put the stock in a saucepan and bring it to the boil, then pour over the potatoes. Dot the top with the remaining butter, then cover the potatoes with the baking parchment and press down. Bake for an hour, then remove the baking parchment. Using the point of a knife, check to make sure the potatoes are tender. Leave the dish in the oven for a further 10 minutes to allow the top layer of potatoes to crisp up and take on some colour.

Unlike Rex Fairbrother, Jill's grandson David has genuine experience with beef cattle. While doing his routine checks this morning, he was pleased to find one of his deep red and white Hereford cows licking her newborn calf. David and Ruth have selectively bred their beef cattle for easy calving, keeping those dams (mothers) who have not needed much help in the past, and who are most likely to bear calves of a suitable shape and size. As a result, most of them get on with it themselves. The rough towelling the calf is receiving is rather like being assailed with damp sandpaper. But it dries it off, warms it up, and stimulates its breathing, circulation and digestive system.

David and Ruth got into high-quality beef production in 2001. They chose Herefords, one of the oldest British breeds, partly because they are friendly and docile, and also because of their ability to convert grass into desirable 'marbled' beef. As the calf starts to feed, David gets back on his quad bike and heads off to take a look at the sheep.

Fallon is not the only one seeking advice from a more experienced head.

'But I've already made my chutney, Emma.'

In the kitchen at Grange Farm, Clarrie is rolling out a football of pastry to something approaching the size of a manhole cover. Feeding the Grundy family requires catering on an industrial scale, as she knows only too well.

'I know,' replies Emma. 'I just want some pointers, that's all.'

'Well, I s'pose I could—'

The kitchen door crashes open.

'What's for tea, Clarrielove?' Eddie carries a plastic bucket full of rich purple berries. You could take them for blueberries but taste one and the sourness would pucker your face.

'You be careful with them sloes. They'll stain.'

'Just going to stick 'em in the freezer. Since Toby Fair-brother's been good enough to give us a bottle of his gin . . .'

Clarrie looks dubious. 'He did what?'

'Well, it were actually in settlement of a debt of hon-our.'

A word of advice. Never play cards with a Grundy.

SLOE GIN
Makes 1.5 litres

500g sloes
250g caster sugar
1 litre gin (or vodka)

Wash the sloes well and pick off any stalks. Dry the berries with kitchen paper, then prick each one a few times with a darning needle. If you don't fancy doing this, you can put the berries in a plastic bag and freeze them for a day or so. This will split the berries so you don't need to prick them.

Pile them into a sterilised 2-litre Kilner jar, or a couple of smaller jars, and add the sugar and the gin. Seal the jar and shake well. For the next few weeks give the mixture a good shake every day and then put the jar away in a cool, dark cupboard for at least 2 months, preferably longer.

When you're ready to use, strain the sloe gin through a muslin-lined sieve and decant into clean bottles.

SEPTEMBER

Eddie is in good spirits, because tomorrow is the start of the turkey-rearing season. A cacophony of screechy chirps will herald the arrival of several dozen six-week-old turkey poults. He and his son Ed Grundy will introduce them to their new straw-baled home in the rough pole barn in Grundy's Field down the road. Pigeon-sized and fluffy now, when fully grown these birds are destined for the Christmas dining tables of Borsetshire, giving the Grundys a useful income at that expensive time of year.

'The judging's finished. You can come back in.' Robert Snell has to nip nimbly sideways to avoid the anxious flood of contenders re-entering the Village Hall. They stream between the white-clothed tables, scanning their entries for the cards that announce this year's victors in the Ambridge Flower and Produce Show. There are plates of five tomatoes, or twelve French beans, uncannily uniform in size and colour. Ten spikes of mixed sweet peas, each a candy-coloured dream. Seven rock buns, some showing the nibbled evidence of the judges' tasting. One entry carries the dreaded mark 'NAS' – Not As Schedule. It has been disqualified for being presented without the required clear covering; a rookie error.

And there on the table near the stage, neatly labelled and snugly lidded, sit the preserves.

Shoulder to shoulder, past the glossy quiches and larger-than-life onions, Emma and Fallon approach their reckoning. Not just their dignity is at stake. Their families have had to endure hours of vacillation over coarseness of chopping, sugar types and spicing. Both houses have reeked for days with the nostril-invading smell of hot vinegar. But this moment . . . this moment is going to make it all worthwhile.

The women survey the table. Three jars have been adorned with the coveted cards. First prize goes to Jill Archer. Second to Clarrie Grundy. Third, Pat Fletcher. Emma and Fallon's efforts have been spurned, unfeted. Not even a Highly Commended.

Emma gives Fallon a look.

'If I'm honest, I was never very keen on chutney anyway.'

'Me neither. Fancy a drink?'

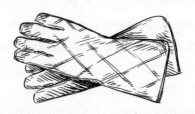

GREEN TOMATO CHUTNEY

Makes about 4 jars

1.5kg green tomatoes
1 litre white wine vinegar
450g brown sugar
1 tsp salt
1 tsp mustard seeds
1 tsp ground ginger
1 tsp ground allspice
1 onion, peeled and finely chopped
200g sultanas

Peel and chop the tomatoes and put them in a large pan with the vinegar, sugar and salt. Cook over a gentle heat until the sugar has dissolved, stirring often, then add the spices, chopped onion and sultanas. Bring to the boil and then simmer for about 2 hours, stirring frequently, until the chutney has a jam-like consistency.

Transfer to sterilised jars and cover with lids or jam-pot covers. Store in a cool, dark place and, if possible, leave for a few weeks before using. Store in the fridge after opening.

CHAPTER TWO

October

I have to warn you, there is a lot of sex in October. And it is described with very direct Middle English words, so buckle up.

'Tup' is both a noun and a verb. It's the old name for a ram, and you will still hear it used in that way. More frequently it is used to describe the act itself. At many farms, including Brookfield, October into November is tupping season.

As the morning sun lances through the mist, giving an ethereal quality to the familiar pastures, David and his younger son Ben drive their bleating ewes. David nods with approval as sheepdog Bess responds fluidly to Ben's commands. A firm 'Come bye!' and Bess moves to the left, clockwise around the flock. 'Away!' means the opposite. When Bess is at a distance, Ben uses the whistle – a curved-sided metal triangle that sits on his tongue. A quick, high double note through the small hole signifies Come Bye, a single mid-tone Away. Now Ben blows a longer, higher blast and Bess immediately drops to the ground, alert and ready for the next command.

These ewes are being placed in various fields depending on their weight. Too skinny and they may not ovulate, but too much fat will bring problems come lambing time. So they will be fed appropriately to bring them all near the ideal tupping weight of about 70 kilograms. This will be a daily job for someone, and they need to be as nimble as Robert Snell in the Village Hall doorway. Keen Flower and

Produce Show contestants are as nothing compared to hungry ewes hearing their dinner tumbling from that large plastic sack into a long metal trough. David has had his legs bowled from under him on more than one occasion.

Ben turns to his father. 'So we're not doing anything for Harvest Supper this year?'

David's face darkens. 'No. Uncle Tony's giving them a side of beef.'

'That's good, isn't it? If we don't have to bother—'

'Because your uncle Kenton reckoned Bridge Farm beef was better than ours.'

'What?!'

'Yeah. Thanks, brother.'

Although theoretically retired from running Bridge Farm, Tony has found it hard to let go completely. In 2019, his family thought he would give up his hobby herd of Angus cattle to make way for the new Montbéliarde dairy herd. Instead, he came up with a plan to sell their meat at the farm shop and direct to customers. It was a blow for Brookfield, who had up to then supplied their Hereford beef to the Bridge Farm shop.

In the yard at Bridge Farm, Johnny is helping his grandfather run the herd through a handling system. Angus cattle turn grass into beef very efficiently, so they are well suited to Bridge Farm's organic system. Tony appraises the glossy black four-square beasts with their distinctive domed heads. He is looking for steers (neutered males) and heifers (females that have not given birth) which have enough 'condition' (essentially, bulk) to be sent for slaughter. Johnny swings the gate left for the abattoir or right for a stay of execution.

<><><><><><><><><><><><><><><><><><><><><><><><><>

Ambridge International

HUNGARY

<><><><><><><><><><><><><><><><><><><><><><><><><>

In 2002, Brian Aldridge invested in an organic farm in Hungary. It infuriated Pat and Tony because up until then Brian had been sniffy at best about organics. But the economics made sense and that is all that mattered for Brian.

After three years, he was ready to increase his involvement in the country and put £100,000 into a British consortium which was buying farms with notional Hungarian partners. It was Debbie and Adam's turn to be annoyed. They were meant to be running Home Farm with Brian, and would have welcomed that sort of investment. Brushing aside their protests, Brian cleverly asked Debbie to visit and report on their latest acquisition. He was so impressed by her findings that he persuaded his partners to offer her a job managing the whole Hungarian operation. This left Adam furious at being sidelined. You would almost think that Brian enjoyed the sight of noses out of joint.

In 2018, Brian had to sell his Hungarian holdings to help pay for the clear-up after the pollution scandal. But it was the start of a new life for Debbie, who grew to love the country and her work there.

HUNGARIAN BEEF GOULASH
Serves 4–6

3 tbsp olive oil

1kg braising steak, cubed

2 large onions, peeled and finely sliced

3 garlic cloves, peeled and finely chopped

1 tbsp plain flour

1 tsp hot paprika

1 tbsp sweet paprika

2 bay leaves

100ml red wine

400g can of tomatoes

300ml beef stock

2 red peppers, deseeded and cut into strips

2 green peppers, deseeded and cut into strips

salt and black pepper

To serve

soured cream

finely chopped parsley

Heat a tablespoon of the oil in a large flameproof casserole dish. Sear the beef over a high heat on all sides, working in at least 2 batches so you don't overcrowd the pan. Add a little more oil for the second batch.

Remove the beef from the casserole dish and add any

remaining oil. Add the onions and cook, again over a high heat, for a few minutes until they start to caramelise around the edges. Sprinkle in the garlic, followed by the flour and paprikas and stir to combine. Put the meat back in the casserole and add the bay leaves.

Pour in the wine and bring to the boil, scraping up any brown bits on the base of the casserole dish as you go, then add the tomatoes and stock. Season with salt and pepper, then bring back to the boil. Cover and turn down to a simmer. Cook over a low heat for 1½ hours, then add the peppers. Continue to cook for another 30 minutes and then check that the beef and the peppers are tender – if they are not, cook for a little longer.

Remove the lid and turn the heat up slightly to reduce the sauce. Stir in a tablespoon of soured cream before serving and sprinkle with parsley. Serve with more soured cream on the side.

Celebrations of the end of harvest exist all round the world. In Britain, the tradition dates back to pre-Christian times and is synonymous with this time of year; literally, given that the Old English word 'haerfest' actually means autumn. A good harvest could mean the difference between life and death. So when everything was safely gathered in, it was usual for the farmer to host a meal to thank everyone who had been involved. 'A meal' makes it sound like a sedate and civilised affair. But we can imagine that the relief after a month of toil, coupled with free food and (especially) drink gave the peasantry licence for the hooliest of hooleys. Imagine the Grundys in full flow, with a side order of Horrobins, and you will get an inkling.

The Ambridge Harvest Supper is a true community affair; lots of people mucking in with the arrangements and the catering. There is usually entertainment of some sort – often a barn dance with the steps called by buxom, buck-skin-clad Jolene Rogers, the one-time Lily of Leyton Cross.

At various times the meal has been held at the Village Hall, Brookfield Farm, Bridge Farm, The Bull, Home Farm, and even in a marquee on the village green. In 1997, it became a truly moveable feast, on 'safari supper' lines. One course was served in each of the surrounding villages: Darrington, Edgeley and Penny Hassett; while in Ambridge, Jennifer Aldridge waited with the desserts she had lovingly created. And waited . . . and waited. She eventually learned that each village had gone so over the top with their catering that most people were stuffed to bursting and could not consume any more. Poor Jennifer!

BLACKBERRY AND APPLE PIE

(freezes well)

Serves 6

500g cooking apples, peeled, cored and sliced

200g blackberries

2 tbsp plain flour

1 tsp cinnamon

½ tsp ground allspice

150g sugar, plus a little extra for sprinkling

1 egg, beaten

Pastry

400g plain flour, plus extra for rolling

50g icing sugar

250g cold butter, cubed

1 egg, beaten

2 tbsp cold water

For the pastry, put the flour and sugar in a food processor and pulse briefly to mix. Add the cubes of butter and pulse until the mixture resembles breadcrumbs. Do not over-process or the pastry will be tough. Tip the mixture into a bowl and add the egg and as much of the water as you need to form a dough. Shape the dough into a ball, then divide it into roughly two-thirds and one-third.

Roll out the larger piece of pastry on a floured work surface until it is a little larger than your pie dish. Use it to line the pie dish, then leave it in the fridge to chill for 20 minutes or so.

Preheat the oven to 200°C/Fan 180°C/Gas 6. Put the apples and blackberries in a bowl with the flour, spices and sugar and mix well. Tip the filling into the pie dish. Brush the rim of the dish with beaten egg.

Roll out the remaining piece of pastry and use it to cover the pie. Trim the pastry if necessary and press the edges of the pastry together to seal, then crimp them with your fingers. Make a small hole in the centre of the pie with a sharp knife to allow steam to escape. If you like, decorate the pie with any pastry trimmings. Brush the top with beaten egg and sprinkle with a little sugar. Bake the pie for about 50 minutes or until cooked through and golden brown. Serve with cream, custard or ice cream.

Poor Joe Grundy too. In 1992, the theme was 'rich man, poor man'. To highlight global inequality, a draw determined whether you would eat well or frugally. Joe's outrage at being served a bowl of rice was only magnified by the sight of Brian Aldridge tucking into a succulent casserole.

Back to tupping. Once the ewes are all in place, it is time to introduce the rams; about one for every fifty ewes. Usually more than one ram is put in with each group, in case one of them is – unfortunate phrase – 'firing blanks'.

With perhaps hundreds of ewes and multiple tups, some system is needed to keep track. This is called 'raddling'. Each ram wears a webbing harness with a block crayon on his chest, which marks the ewe when he mounts her. David changes the colour every week, so he knows not only that the ewes have been 'served', but also the order in which they are likely to give birth in the spring.

It used to be a messier business. Raddling, that is; the brisk, unromantic process of sheep lovemaking is pretty much the same as it ever was. As an alternative to the harness arrangement, many farmers still make their own raddle by mixing coloured powder with oil and smearing it on the ram's chest and belly. This has been going on a long time. A key character in Thomas Hardy's 1878 novel *The Return of the Native* is Diggory Venn, whose diabolical red-stained skin trumpets his profession of 'reddleman'. In 2015, Toby Fairbrother appeared to make his own diabolical bid for that title when he chucked purple raddle into Home Farm's swimming pool. He thought it was funny, which probably tells you all you need to know about Toby Fairbrother.

'You all right for the twenty-first? . . . Edward?'

'Sorry, what?'

At Grange Farm, Eddie Grundy finds his son surveying the flock of pedigree Texel sheep. Like David and Ben, Ed is preoccupied with tupping too, but it is on a smaller scale and a more precision affair. With their distinctive wide faces and forward-cocked ears, Texels are one of the meatiest of breeds. But meat is not the prime purpose of Ed's flock. He wants to generate high-quality offspring, with excellent ratings for all the important breed characteristics. A top-performing ram will sell for thousands of pounds, because of the sheer number of lambs he could sire in his lifetime.

'You'll have a few champions in there, don't you worry,' Eddie assures him.

Ed works hard to maximise his chances of producing an animal that will garner rosettes at agricultural shows. He tries to rise above the fact that his niece Poppy christened his first prize-winning ram 'Peppa Pig'.

'Just don't forget Apple Day, will you?'

Apple Day falls on 21 October. Ah, that traditional celebration of the quintessential English fruit, its origins lost in the mists of – Oh . . . no, as you were. Actually, Apple Day was invented in 1990 by the conservation charity Common Ground. Do not confuse it with Oak Apple Day (29 May), which dates back to the restoration of King Charles II in 1660. Ambridge has enthusiastically adopted the young upstart – led by the Grundys, who have parlayed it into a manufacturing and marketing opportunity for their infamous cider.

TOFFEE APPLES
Makes 8

8 eating apples
120g golden syrup
225g golden caster sugar
1 tsp vinegar

Wash the apples and dry them well. Remove their stalks and push a lolly stick or wooden skewer into the stalk end. Place the apples on a baking tray lined with baking parchment. Put the syrup, sugar and vinegar in a pan with 100ml of water and place the pan over a medium heat. Cook for about 5 minutes until the sugar has dissolved, stirring constantly, then bring to the boil. Boil until the mixture reaches 150°C. If you don't have a thermometer, put a drop of the liquid into a bowl of cold water and if it hardens and becomes brittle, it's ready.

Remove the pan from the heat and quickly dip in an apple. Twist it to make sure it is coated all over, then place it on the baking sheet. Repeat to coat the rest of the apples and then leave them to set. Take care – the toffee mixture will be very, very hot!

Fleeing Russia's oncoming winter, a small flock of field-fares has settled at Home Farm. The birds provide a chuckling counterpoint to a mournful bassline. Those cries, like a moo from the biggest and angriest cow you might ever meet, are the sound of the rut.

Deer are relatively low-maintenance animals and, if you can put up with the racket every autumn, they are also quite picturesque. In fact, when Brian introduced them to Home Farm in 1987, an ice cream van arrived to service the gawping crowds. Brian soon chased them off. He was a bit of a young buck himself in those days, although we are mixing our deer metaphors here, as a 'buck' is a male fallow deer. Home Farm's stags – male red deer – live together peacefully for most of the year. But in the autumn the testosterone flows. They compete through aggressive displays, and sometimes antler-clashing fights, to become one of the small number who will dominate the mating season. It's much like the centre of Felpersham on a Saturday night.

Adam mainly lets the stags and hinds get on with it. Just as well, because he too has sheep who are tupping away merrily, and it is time for one of the most fraught tasks of the year: the maize harvest. The Estate grows a lot of maize. Combined with the effluent from the Berrow Farm pig unit, it feeds an anaerobic digester which powers the unit and supplies electricity to the National Grid.

Concerned with soil health as he is, Adam is not keen on maize. Its tall, widely spaced plants leave the ground exposed through the growing season. And because it is a marginal crop for the British climate, it is harvested very late – the last harvest of the year. By early October, the ground is often wet. The rocket-shaped teeth of the maize harvester give it the menacing appearance of a missile launcher in a Red Square parade. Its toing and froing (along with the tractors which collect the chopped crop) can compact the soil, especially if it is waterlogged. It can leave this precious resource vulnerable through the winter to flooding and run-off into rivers and drains.

At Home Farm, Adam has started to sow ryegrass between the rows of maize, so that the soil is not left exposed to the rain. One obvious benefit is that the machines leave less mud on the roads than during the Estate's maize harvest. Adam is often not a popular chap at this time of year. But he and his team have to tough it out as they work late into the night, the chilly darkness moderated by the banks of lights set above their cab windscreens.

Meanwhile at Bridge Farm, things are happening on a more human scale. Tom is planting oriental greens for winter salads – pak choi, mizuna, mustard leaves. Occasionally he takes refuge from the increasingly bleak weather to plan next year's planting, scrolling through the websites of seed suppliers. Outside, the trees gently disrobe, by the end of the month reduced to gaunt skeletons.

The carrots are harvested in a similar manner to last month's potatoes, earthed up by a tractor-towed 'bed lifter', and bunched into dozens by the followers. Like the spuds, the carrots are put in store and will be drawn on through the winter. In contrast, swedes, turnips and cabbages are pulled by hand one row at a time as needed – as is that great winter staple of the Bridge Farm veg boxes, the noble leek.

LEEK AND POTATO SOUP

Serves 6

50g butter
1 onion, peeled and chopped
2 large leeks, washed and sliced
2 celery sticks, chopped
400g potatoes, peeled and diced
1.2 litres vegetable stock
1 bay leaf
parsley stalks, chopped
salt and black pepper

To serve
single cream or crème fraiche
chopped parsley leaves

Melt the butter in a large pan and add the onion, leeks, celery and potatoes. Stir well to coat the veg in the butter, then cover the pan and leave to cook gently for 10 minutes or so. Keep checking and stirring and don't allow the vegetables to brown.

Add the stock, bay leaf and parsley stalks, season with salt and pepper, then bring to the boil. Cover the pan and leave the soup to simmer for 30 minutes until all the vegetables are nice and tender.

Remove the pan from the heat and allow the soup to cool

slightly. Take out the bay leaf and blitz the soup with a stick blender or in a food processor until you have the texture you desire.

Serve with a swirl of cream or crème fraiche and garnish with parsley.

Ed ties one of Clarrie's scarves snugly around Tilly Button's head. 'Come on then, round you go!' He spins the girl, who wobbles towards a rudimentary painting of an apple on an upright board.

'Pin the Maggot on the Apple!' he cries. 'Two goes for a pound!'

Apple Day has arrived, and the Grundys are milking it for every penny. The field at Grange Farm resembles a very single-minded village fete, hosting a bucket of pomaceous activities.

The spluttering and squeals nearby are from Poppy Grundy, hands behind her back, chasing fugitive fruit round Clarrie's water-filled washing up bowl. We hear an anguished moan as Ben Archer's knife slips, ruining his attempt in the Longest Peel competition. And, of course, there is apple-y food in abundance – for a very reasonable price.

SAUSAGE AND APPLE ROLLS

Serves 4–6

500g sausage meat or skinned sausages
2 apples, peeled and finely diced
1 tsp chopped thyme leaves
½ tsp chopped sage
500g puff pastry
flour, for dusting
1 egg, beaten
salt and black pepper

Preheat the oven to 200°C/Fan 180°C/Gas 6. Mix the sausage meat with the diced apple and the herbs, then season well with salt and pepper.

Roll out the pastry on a floured surface and cut it into 2 long rectangles, measuring about 18cm wide. Divide the sausage mixture in half and place a roll of it down the middle of one of the rectangles of pastry. Brush one edge of the pastry with beaten egg, fold it over the sausage filling and press to seal. Crimp the edges nicely with a fork and brush with beaten egg. Repeat with the rest of the pastry and filling.

Cut each roll into individual sausage rolls, as big or small as you like. Cut a small slash in each one. Bake for 15–20 minutes or until the filling is cooked and the pastry is beautifully crisp and brown. Delicious hot or cold.

A metallic clatter shocks the chattering crowd into silence. Eddie is beating an old tin tray with a spanner.

'Right you lot,' he calls. 'All members of the cider club – and anyone who wants to join – time for the Grand Gathering.'

Eddie leads a ragged procession to Grange Farm's ancient orchard – a community asset since 2012. Everyone sets to, shaking the branches with sticks and loading the fallen Borsetshire Beauties, Kingston Blacks and other varieties into old feed sacks.

Being sharp of eye, you will notice in the orchard a couple of interlopers among the apple and pear trees. Their fruit is pear-shaped (in a good way), but of a more golden hue than any pear could dream. They are quinces, and they are ready for picking now, before the first frosts. Don't be tempted to bite into a raw one; they are as hard and tart as a knock-back from Tracy Horrobin. Cooked, though, is another matter . . .

This is usually served to accompany the cheeseboard.

QUINCE JELLY
Makes about 6 jars

2.5kg quinces
sugar (450g per 600ml
  of juice)

zest and juice of
1 lemon

Wash the quinces well and remove any damaged parts. Cut them up and put them in a pan with enough water to come just level with the fruit. Bring to the boil, then turn down the heat and leave to simmer until the fruit is soft. Tip everything into a jelly bag or a muslin-lined sieve over a bowl and leave overnight.

The next day put a couple of saucers in the freezer for checking the set. Pour the quince juice into a measuring jug, then into a clean pan and add 450g of sugar per 600ml of juice. Add the lemon zest and juice, then bring to the boil, stirring frequently. Check that all the sugar has dissolved, then you can start checking the set of the jelly.

Put a small amount of the jelly on a cold saucer and if it wrinkles when gently pushed with your finger, it is ready. If not, continue to boil for a few more moments and then test again. When the jelly is ready, pour it into warm sterilised jars and seal. It will keep for months, but store opened jars in the fridge.

The cider-making process has not changed for decades. In fact, about the only difference between now and a hundred years ago is that many of the vessels used are plastic. Once the apples are collected, willing hands roughly chop them, and the pieces are pulped by a noisy 'scratter'. The Grundys' scratter is purpose-built, but some people make their own, even adapting garden shredders.

The apple pulp is carried in buckets to the nearby press (oddly reminiscent of a medieval instrument of torture) and wrapped in hessian to form a 'cheese'. A screw handle is turned by good old-fashioned muscle power and the air is soon filled with the sweet aroma of apple juice. The Grundys would never admit this, but the process of making farmhouse cider is actually pretty simple, mainly requiring patience. Over the next few weeks, natural yeasts turn the sugar in the juice to alcohol. Once this fermentation is finished, the cider is left to mature for about six months, until ready for consumption.

Behind the Scenes

In an interesting coincidence, Brian Hewlett – the actor who plays veteran pigman Neil Carter – is a member of a very similar community cider club in his home village in East Anglia. Here is a recipe which brings both tasty products together.

PORK IN CIDER
Serves 4–6

3 tbsp olive oil
15g butter
2 onions, peeled and sliced
2 celery sticks, roughly chopped
3 carrots, peeled and roughly chopped
1 tbsp plain flour
1 tsp mustard powder
750g braising pork, diced
500ml dry cider
2 bay leaves
a few small rosemary sprigs
1 tbsp wholegrain mustard
50ml single cream (optional)
salt and black pepper

Heat a tablespoon of the oil and the butter in a large flameproof casserole dish. When the butter has melted and foamed, add the onions, celery and carrots. Sauté over a medium heat until the vegetables have started to soften and caramelise around the edges.

Mix the flour with the mustard powder and some salt and pepper. Toss this mixture with the pork, dusting off any excess. Heat another tablespoon of the oil in a large frying pan, sear the pork on all sides, then add it to the casserole. You will probably have to do this in 2 batches – use the remaining oil for the second batch if so.

Add half the cider to the frying pan and bring it to the boil to deglaze, scraping up any brown bits on the bottom of the pan. Pour all of this over the contents of the casserole dish, then add the rest of the cider, the herbs and the wholegrain mustard.

Bring to the boil, then turn down the heat and cover. Simmer for 1–1½ hours, then remove the lid and leave the sauce to reduce down for another 30 minutes. By this time the pork and vegetables should be tender. Pour in the single cream, if using, and simmer for another minute or so. Serve with mashed potatoes.

'Cheers, lad.' Two earthenware mugs are bumped together as Ed and Eddie sample the latest vintage. 'That's us sorted for the year.'

Since the cider club was established, there have been various ways of calculating what proportion the Grundys keep for themselves, and how much labour qualifies club members for what quantity of cider. But the stuff is so strong that once they've quaffed a couple a pints no one cares much anyway.

'Cheers, Dad. Fancy a top-up?'

CHAPTER THREE

November

Climate change can throw curveballs at us. But if November plays according to type, its days can be as grey as a banker's suit. As the temperatures drop steadily through the month, we can expect an average of only three hours of sunshine daily. Yes, British Summer Time has most definitely ended. Although for farmers that is not as grim a transition as it is for many urban dwellers. To the townie, the clocks going back at the end of October can slam like a prison door on the first day of a gloomy five-month sentence. But farmers tend to get up earlier than most of us, so for a while they get a brighter hour at the start of their day.

The bleak weather has not deterred retired professor Jim Lloyd from his passion for birdwatching. Binoculars on chest, he is returning from a morning walk. For much of the bird population, this is a time of coming of age. Young blackbirds and robins may head south-west. More clingy ones will be chased away by their parents to find local lodgings. Mother of daughters Sabrina Thwaite wishes she was as ruthless when faced yet again with a bedroom full of festering laundry, dotted with cereal-encrusted dishes, and mugs in which the successor to penicillin may one day be discovered.

As Jim takes out his front door key, he notes the thrushes feasting on the exuberant, tightly packed red berries of a hawthorn. The music of the mistle and song thrushes rather outdoes the redwings and fieldfares which arrived last month, but Jim welcomes them all.

'Morning, prof.'

Jim turns to see Eddie Grundy, a furry corpse dangling casually from one hand.

'Thought you might fancy this for the pot. Free of charge.'

Jim raises a cynical eyebrow. 'Poached rabbit?'

Eddie appears deeply offended. 'Not poached. Totally legit, honest. They been getting into Adam's barley, so I been over there with me ferrets.'

'Sorry, Eddie, I wouldn't know what to do with it.'

'I'll prep it for you, if you like.'

Jim waits for the catch. Eddie stands there, a picture of neighbourliness.

'All right, then. Come in.'

With Jim keeping half an eye through the kitchen window, hoping for the return of a green woodpecker, the whole animal is quickly transformed into joints ready for cooking.

'There you go.' Eddie rinses his fine-bladed knife under the tap.

'Thank you. That's very kind of you.'

'No problem. Now, while I'm here . . . Have you thought about Christmas yet?'

Later, bemused Jim is dredging the joints with flour ready for browning. You have to hand it to the Grundys, he thinks. Somehow, Eddie exchanged one rabbit, caught free of charge at Home Farm, for a £60 turkey order. Mind you, he was armed with a knife.

Ambridge International

GERMANY

◇◇◇◇◇◇◇◇◇◇◇◇◇◇◇◇◇◇◇◇◇◇◇◇◇◇◇◇◇◇◇◇◇◇◇◇◇◇

In 1995, the Grundys were temporarily evacuated when the wreckage of a wartime German aircraft was discovered in boggy ground in one of their fields. It brought back memories for Joe Grundy, and for retired gamekeeper Tom Forrest. During the war, the two men had been first on the scene when the aeroplane crashed, and they detained the pilot until the authorities arrived.

They had not realised that another body was on board, undiscovered until now: that of the gunner Hubert Weisner. After all these years, Weisner's daughter requested that he be buried in the village where he had died. Tom was initially very opposed to the idea. He feared that once you forgive, you start to forget. But he was eventually persuaded to attend the funeral and met the pilot he had captured fifty years before, a Herr Hemsal. To see the two old men put past enmity behind them and embrace was very moving.

HASENPFEFFER – GERMAN RABBIT CASSEROLE

Serves 4

1 rabbit, jointed into 6–8 pieces

250ml red wine

150ml red wine vinegar

2 garlic cloves, finely chopped

2 pieces of pared lemon zest

1 bouquet garni (2 bay leaves, 2 rosemary sprigs, 1 thyme
   sprig, 2 parsley sprigs)

1 tsp juniper berries, lightly crushed

1 tsp black peppercorns, lightly crushed

2 cloves

2 tbsp lard or olive oil

2 tbsp flour

100g streaky bacon, cut into strips

2 onions, peeled and thickly sliced

200ml chicken stock or water

100ml soured cream

salt and black pepper

Put the rabbit joints in a non-metallic bowl. Put the wine,
vinegar, garlic, lemon zest, bouquet garni and spices into a
pan and bring to the boil. Remove the pan from the heat and
leave to cool, then when the marinade is at room temperature,
pour it over the rabbit. Put the bowl in the fridge and leave to
marinate for several hours at least or up to 2 days.

When you are ready to cook, remove the bowl from the fridge and let the rabbit come up to room temperature.

Heat the lard or oil in a large flameproof casserole dish. Remove the rabbit pieces from the marinade and pat dry thoroughly. Dust with the flour and pat off any excess, then fry the pieces in the casserole until lightly browned – you will probably have to do this in a couple of batches.

Remove the rabbit from the casserole dish and add the bacon and onions. Cook them over a medium heat until the bacon is crisp and brown, then pour in the marinade, together with the stock or water. Bring to the boil, stirring constantly to scrape up any brown bits on the base of the dish, then season with plenty of salt. Put the rabbit back in the casserole and cover. Simmer until the meat is tender – this will take at least an hour, probably an hour and a half.

Once the rabbit is tender, remove it from the casserole dish and keep it warm. Turn up the heat to reduce the cooking liquor by half. Ladle some out and whisk it with the soured cream, then stir this mixture back into the casserole dish. Taste for seasoning and spoon the sauce over the rabbit.

NOVEMBER

For the farmers of Ambridge, it is the dampness of November that raises the greatest challenges. This is a key time of transition for Bridge Farm and Brookfield. At the start of the month, both have their cattle out in their fields. By the end, most of them will be housed indoors. The big question is, when to bring them in?

At Bridge Farm Johnny is in Long Meadow, gazing thoughtfully at the dairy herd. Montbéliardes are officially a red pied breed. 'Pied' in this case just means two-coloured, originally in reference to the black and white of the magpie. Each one displays a unique coat of random white and red-brown patches. They are good-looking beasts. But at the moment Johnny is more concerned about the ground on which they are grazing.

With the reducing temperatures and elusive sunshine, the grass is getting dangerously low. And the more rain that falls, the more the horny, cloven hooves of the cattle will 'poach' the soil into mud. They must be moved into their winter housing before the ground is damaged, or it will not provide the high-quality grass they will need come the spring. But as soon as they are inside, Bridge Farm's costs will effectively rise, as the cows will be housed on straw, eating silage.

'What do you think, then? Tony joins his grandson in the gateway. 'How much longer?'

'I were going to ask you, Grandad.'

Tony does not really get on with the 'Monteys'. For him, they have too much Gallic obstinacy. But he knows his land and has been checking the weather forecast.

'We'll probably be all right for another week.'

Perhaps a fortnight after that, Tony will bring in his suckler herd of Angus cattle. A suckler herd is pretty much what it sounds like: cows who are still feeding their calves, although it must be said that by now these are pretty big calves. He will need a few helpers, so most of the family will turn out: someone leading, another driving them from the rear, plus a couple of stoppers in the yard, to make sure they don't make a break for it and end up among the mismatched vintage crockery in Fallon's tearoom. The temptation to make a bull in a china shop joke here is almost irresistible . . .

At Brookfield, Pip, David and Ruth go through a similarly anxious process. Although their timings might be a little different, the principle is the same. One evening after milking, rather than being walked back to the field, the dairy cows will find themselves directed into a strawed-down barn, their quarters for the next five months. And within a few weeks, the Herefords will be brought in too. But not all of them. They will leave some youngstock (a term which covers anything from a calf to a heifer about to give birth) in the fields all winter. The Hereford is a hardy breed, perfectly able to 'outwinter'. But any animal that is in the final stages of fattening is best brought under cover, so they can use their energy to put on condition, rather than keeping themselves warm against the chill winds and frosts of December.

'I had a few old pallets, so I dumped them on the green.'

Although this sounds like fly-tipping, David is actually rather pleased at the news.

'Thanks, Eddie. Any chance of helping me build it?'

David often finds himself responsible for the village bonfire. Although the 5 November celebrations were traditionally held on the village green, since 2012 they have sometimes been relocated to Jubilee Field. This small patch by the river was donated to the village as a 'field in trust' for the Queen's Diamond Jubilee. Whatever the location, some lucky person has to go around scaring up donations of bonfire wood, then someone (often the same person) has to build it. Most importantly someone has to check it for sheltering wildlife before it is lit. In 2001, Lynda Snell liberated a toad from certain incineration, and in 2006 Ben and Josh Archer found a hedgehog. They were allowed to keep it for one night only, before returning it to the wild. But that didn't stop them giving it the incredibly original name of Spiky.

'Yeah, I could probably spare you an hour or so.'

'Brilliant. Thanks a lot.'

'Now, David. Have you thought about Christmas yet?'

Eddie never misses a chance, does he?

The fireworks are funded by public subscription or business donation, so the event is usually free. But you can always spend money if you wish. Before Tom sold it, the Gourmet Grills food van used to be a regular fixture, but The Bull really sees Bonfire Night as its territory. This is why Kenton and Jolene argue very strongly to keep it on the green, which is a Catherine wheel's spin from the pub.

As well as encouraging people to make a night of it in the bar, they usually serve food outside. The fare varies from year to year, but two staples are never absent. As far back as 1984, *The Archers* archive records the then landlord Sid Perks serving bangers in jacket potatoes – sausages, that is, not the firework. And, of course, there is always that traditional tooth-binding honeycomb known as cinder toffee.

On the Menu – The Bull

CINDER TOFFEE

butter, for greasing
100g granulated sugar
45g golden syrup
1 tsp bicarbonate of soda

Grease a baking tin with butter and line it with greased baking parchment. Put the sugar and syrup in a heavy-based pan and heat slowly until the sugar has melted. Stir frequently and keep a close eye on the mixture so it doesn't burn. Check the temperature with a sugar thermometer and once it has reached 150°C continue to boil for about 10 minutes until the toffee is a beautiful golden colour.

Take the pan off the heat and whisk in the bicarb. Take care, as the mixture will bubble up ferociously. Pour the toffee into the tin and leave to cool, then break it up into pieces.

Ambridge is relatively unusual in retaining the tradition of burning a guy, which has led to some amusing incidents over the years. In 2014, when the village was up in arms at Borchester Land's proposal to drive a new road through a large swathe of the village, the guy bore a notable resemblance to Justin Elliott. And way back in 1952, Peggy Woolley's mother Polly Perkins had palpitations when she came across Dan Archer (David's grandfather), apparently either dead drunk or having had an accident of some sort. This was because Walter Gabriel had dressed the guy in some of Dan's old clothes. Poor old Mrs P had to take a drop of medicinal brandy for her nerves.

Behind the Scenes

When *The Archers* began in 1951, the production secretary Valerie Hodgetts started to keep records of storylines, characters and locations on file index cards. When they were finally transferred to computer in the 1990s, there were over 20,000 of them. Although now the production and writing team can access the digitised archive from their desks, we still have those precious original records in their well-worn wooden cabinets.

November is also the month in which the deer rut and the sheep-tupping season end for another year. The exhausted males are separated from the (hopefully) pregnant females. Well done, chaps. Time for a rest. Home Farm's shepherd Eli gives the rams a bit of hay and feed (very quietly; you do not hear much from Eli).

Meanwhile, a line of drably garbed figures enters a copse at the far end of the field. Some tap the trees with sticks, uttering high-pitched trills. Others wave square white flags on short wooden poles. The air beyond the copse suddenly comes alive with a percussive cadenza. The pheasant-shooting season is well under way. Every ten days or so until the end of January, this scene will be repeated in numerous locations around Home Farm, the Berrow Estate, Brookfield and the country park near Grey Gables. The combined shoot is run by Borchester Land, for many years under the day-to-day management of Will Grundy.

Shooting has been a lifelong passion for Brian Aldridge. With the disgrace of his prosecution for land pollution, one of the bitterest pills was having to step back from overseeing shoot operations. That he was supplanted by Martyn Gibson, his persistent rival on the Borchester Land board, twisted the knife still further.

This ignominy also affected Jennifer, as she lost her role as principal caterer for the lunches on shoot days, a job she loved. The big kitchen at Home Farm was perfectly suited to turning out warming, filling British classics. These were just the thing to restore the spirits of a tweed-clad 'gun' after a morning in the cold (and often wet), and to send them out refreshed for the final drives of the day. It is rather frowned upon to serve pheasant or partridge at a shoot lunch, being seen as carrying economy a little far. But no one ever complained about Jennifer's hearty stew, rich with Home Farm venison.

HUNTER'S CASSEROLE
Serves 6

3 tbsp vegetable oil

1.5kg boned leg or shoulder of venison, cut into 3cm cubes

2 tbsp plain flour

250g streaky bacon, chopped

2 onions, peeled and sliced

2 celery sticks, sliced

2 carrots, peeled and diced

500ml red wine

250ml chicken stock

6 juniper berries

2 bay leaves

1 tsp fresh thyme leaves, chopped

1 strip of orange peel

2 tbsp redcurrant jelly

salt and black pepper

Heat 2 tablespoons of the oil in a large flameproof casserole dish. Dust the venison with flour and season it with salt and pepper. Add the meat to the casserole dish and brown it all over – it's best to do this in batches so you don't overcrowd the dish. Once all the venison is browned, set it aside. Preheat the oven to 180°C/Fan 160°C/Gas 4.

Add another tablespoon of oil to the dish and cook the bacon, onions, celery and carrots until softened. Put the venison back in the pan and add the wine, stock, juniper berries, herbs, orange peel and redcurrant jelly. Season with salt and pepper and stir well, then bring to a simmer. Put a lid on the dish, transfer it to the oven and cook for about 2 hours until the venison is beautifully tender.

Taste the juices and add more seasoning if necessary. If the stew seems too liquid, put the casserole dish on the hob and simmer, uncovered, until the gravy has thickened to your liking. Serve with mashed potatoes and greens.

At the end of the day, regardless of how many birds have been shot, each gun takes home a brace of pheasants. The bulk of the remainder will go to a game dealer, but it is not unknown for beaters to get a bird or two as well. If so rewarded, Chris Carter has a simple pan-fry recipe. But sometimes he can persuade his mother Susan to make something a little more elaborate.

AMBRIDGE GAME PIE
Serves 6–8

450g pork, diced
450g boned, diced pheasant or pigeon
450g cooked ham, diced
2 shallots, finely chopped
2 tbsp redcurrant jelly
4 tbsp Madeira
3 tbsp chopped parsley
1 tbsp chopped thyme
½ tsp freshly grated nutmeg
½ tsp ground allspice
1 egg, beaten, to glaze
salt and black pepper

Hot-water crust pastry
450g plain flour, plus extra for dusting
1 tsp salt
200g lard, plus extra for greasing

First make the filling. Put the meats, shallots, redcurrant jelly, Madeira, herbs and spices in a bowl, season with salt and pepper and mix until thoroughly combined. Put the filling in the fridge while you make the pastry.

For the pastry, sift the flour and salt into a bowl. Put the lard in a pan, add 200ml of water and heat until just boiling. Make a well in the flour, then tip in the lard mixture and stir. Mix well, then turn the dough out onto a floured work surface and knead until smooth. Preheat the oven to 200°C/Fan 180°C/Gas 6. Grease a loaf tin or a 20cm springform cake tin.

Divide the pastry into two-thirds and one-third. Roll out the larger piece and use it to line the tin. Spoon in the filling mixture and press it down lightly.

Brush the edges of the pastry with beaten egg, then roll out the remaining pastry and put it on top of the pie. Make a small hole in the top to release steam. Bake the pie for 20 minutes, then turn the heat down to 180°C/Fan 160°C/Gas 4 and cook for another 1½ hours.

Leave the pie to cool completely in the tin, then turn out and serve with pickles.

Pickled onions make a perfect accompaniment to a slice of cold pie. They are made with the button or pickling varieties which are plentiful at this time of year. If made now, they will be ready to bring a bit of zing to the traditional cold collation on Boxing Day. There is fierce argument as to who makes the best pickled onions in Ambridge. Clarrie Grundy's – served sometimes with bread and cheese at the cider club – are a strong contender.

PICKLED ONIONS
Makes 2 big jars

1kg pickling onions
150g salt
600ml malt vinegar
55g sugar
2 tsp black peppercorns
1 tsp coriander seeds
2 tsp mustard seeds
2 cloves
1 bay leaf

Put the onions in a bowl and pour boiling water over them. Leave them for about a minute, then drain and rinse in cold water. Peel off the skins, then put the onions back in the bowl, sprinkle with the salt and cover with cold water. Set aside for 24 hours.

Put the vinegar in a pan with the sugar, spices and bay leaf. Bring to the boil and boil for 5 minutes, then remove the pan from the heat and set the mixture aside to cool completely.

Rinse the onions and dry them with kitchen paper. Pile them into sterilised Kilner jars, then pour in the vinegar and spices to cover. Seal the jars and leave for at least 4 weeks before eating. Store in the fridge after opening.

NOVEMBER

. . . Stir up, O Lord, the wills of your faithful people, that they, bringing forth the fruit of good works, may by you be richly rewarded . . .

So begins the collect (daily prayer) listed in the Book of Common Prayer for the last Sunday before Advent. And as this day falls between 20 and 26 November, it serves as a reminder that it is time to make your Christmas puddings, cakes and mincemeat, as these seasonal treats benefit from several weeks' maturing time. At Brookfield, Jill has done her very best to keep the tradition going – not just as a matter of culinary good practice, but as a family event. Some of the earliest memories that Pip, Josh and Ben can recall are of standing on a chair in the steamy kitchen, a wooden spoon clutched in tiny hands. As David and his siblings did before them, they strained to stir the sticky mixture, each making a wish for the future.

MINCEMEAT

Makes about 6 jars

225g sultanas
350g raisins
350g currants
100g mixed peel
400g dark brown sugar
400g apples, peeled, cored and chopped
300g shredded suet
zest and juice of 1 lemon
zest and juice of 1 orange
a few rasps of nutmeg
½ tsp cinnamon
100ml brandy

Put all the ingredients in a big bowl and mix well. Cover and leave overnight. The next day, stir again, spoon into sterilised jars and cover. Store in a cool dark place and leave for at least 3 weeks, if possible, before using.

As the children passed through the less-dutiful teenage years into young adulthood, it became harder to enthuse them with the entire process. But they usually appear some time during the day to make their wish. Jill always pops an old silver sixpence into the pudding mixture. Extra luck for whoever finds it in their portion on Christmas Day – as long as they do not swallow it, anyway.

CHRISTMAS PUDDING
Makes 1 large or 2 small puddings

55g plain flour, sifted

1 tsp mixed spice

1 tsp ground cinnamon

½ tsp grated nutmeg

110g shredded suet

110g dark brown sugar

100g grated apple

100g grated carrot

225g raisins

110g sultanas

110g currants

110g candied peel

100g glacé cherries, quartered

55g chopped almonds

55g prunes or dried figs, chopped

grated zest and juice of 1 large lemon

1 tbsp black treacle or molasses

140ml Guinness

2 tbsp brandy

110g breadcrumbs

2 eggs, beaten

butter, for greasing

Mix all the ingredients, except the eggs and butter, in a large bowl and stir thoroughly. Cover the bowl and leave overnight for the flavours to mature. The next day, add the eggs and mix well. If the mixture seems too dry, add a little more Guinness to get a soft dropping consistency.

Grease a large pudding basin (or 2 smaller ones) with butter. Line the base with a circle of greaseproof paper. Pile the mixture into the bowl and cover with a circle of greaseproof paper. Take a piece of foil and make a pleat in the middle, then cover the bowl and tie securely with string.

Put a folded tea towel in the base of a large pan, add the pudding basin and pour in boiling water to come halfway up the sides. Steam the pudding for 6–7 hours, keeping a check on the water level and adding more boiling water as necessary.

After steaming, remove the foil and greaseproof paper and add new coverings. Store the pudding in a cool, dark place. On Christmas Day, steam as before for at least an hour, then serve with brandy butter and custard or cream.

Only a small minority of the population attend church nowadays and indeed many folk simply toss a cellophane-wrapped pudding and a jar of mincemeat into the super-market trolley, so there was a danger of the Stir-up Sunday tradition dying out. It is nice to know that some people first heard about it in *The Archers* and have adopted it as their own family ritual.

That's public service broadcasting for you . . .

CHAPTER FOUR
December

'Three, two, one . . . Go!'

The lights adorning The Bull's black and white frontage snap on, and the gloomy beer garden is instantly transformed. On either side, Woodbine Cottage and the Village Hall illuminate simultaneously. The light cascades round all the buildings surrounding the village green. As the 'executive homes' of Glebelands join the former council houses of The Green to complete the circle of light, Kenton returns to the microphone. He speaks over the cheers of the crowd, competing with Hollerton Silver Band's energetic rendition of 'Rudolph the Red-Nosed Reindeer'.

'We've still got plenty of food, and we're open 'til eleven, so do stick around, people.'

'People?' Kenton's nephew Josh gives him a sardonic look. 'Like, for real, man.'

'Shut up, you. How's your mince pie?'

'Not bad. Gran's are better.'

The lights switch-on is Ambridge's way of kicking off the Christmas season, heralding a month of parties, family reunions and present-buying panic. But along with the festive atmosphere can come some pretty tough weather. Sleet, snow, driving rain, hard frosts . . . After November's baleful overture, by December we definitely know that winter has arrived. There is not much sitting in a warm tractor cab at this time of year, so when farmers are out and about they are well layered up in thermals and fleeces. The kitchen Aga or Rayburn serves an additional purpose as dryer of waterlogged outer layers.

Toughened by a lifetime on the land, Bert Fry does not let cold weather keep him from his garden. With the Christmas lights a day-old memory, he is in his store shed, selecting an accompaniment for tonight's main course. The dying sunshine barely makes it through the faded window as he reaches up to a slatted wooden shelf. He already has a colander half full of Brussels sprouts. Now he removes a makeshift blanket, improvised from past issues of the *Borchester Echo*, and takes down a shiny-veined, claret-hued globe.

BRAISED RED CABBAGE
Serves 8

2 tbsp olive oil
2 onions, peeled and thinly sliced
1kg red cabbage, cored and shredded
3 eating apples, peeled, cored and chopped
35g dark brown sugar
3 tbsp cider vinegar
1 bay leaf
1 cinnamon stick
a few cloves
red wine or cider
salt and black pepper

DECEMBER

Heat the olive oil in a flameproof casserole dish, then add the onions and cook until softened but not browned. Add the cabbage and stir well, then leave it to cook for about 15 minutes. Preheat the oven to 160°C/Fan 140°C/Gas 3.

Add the apples, sugar, vinegar, bay leaf, spices and a splash of red wine or cider and stir well. Season with salt and black pepper. Put a lid on the casserole dish and put it in the oven for about an hour. Remove the dish, give everything a stir and add a little more wine or cider if the mixture looks too dry. Check the flavour too and make sure the cabbage isn't too sweet or sour – add a little more vinegar or sugar as necessary. Cook for another 30 minutes, then serve.

This dish is even better the next day, so make ahead if you like and reheat gently before serving.

Sprouts are very much on the agenda at Bridge Farm too, as is that other Christmas veg box essential: parsnips. Tom pulls them and other roots as needed, calling on Johnny's help when he is not busy with the Montbéliardes. Helen is indoors, but she is not particularly warm either, as the dairy is kept cool for food safety reasons. Well wrapped up under her white coat, she and Susan are making one of their seasonal specialities.

FESTIVE ICE CREAM
Serves 8–10

75g raisins
75g sultanas
25g candied peel
50g glacé cherries, halved
50g no-soak dried apricots
2 balls of stem ginger in syrup, diced
6 tbsp brandy
1 tsp mixed spice
3 eggs, plus 2 extra yolks
125g golden caster sugar
300ml single cream
300ml double cream
50g flaked almonds, lightly toasted

Put the dried fruit, cherries, apricots and stem ginger in a pan, then add the brandy and mixed spice. Place over a gentle heat and bring to simmer for 2 minutes, then remove from the heat and leave to cool.

Beat the eggs and egg yolks in a bowl, add the sugar and beat again until pale. Heat the single cream to just below boiling point, then whisk it into the egg mixture. Pour the custard back into the pan and heat gently, stirring constantly, until it thickens and coats the back of a wooden spoon. Pour the custard into a bowl and leave to cool.

Whip the double cream and fold it gently into the custard, then fold in the cooled fruit. Line a freezer-proof container with cling film, leaving plenty hanging over the edges. Pour the mixture into the container and freeze.

To serve, remove the ice cream from the freezer 15–20 minutes before you want to eat it. Turn it out on to a serving plate and remove the cling film, then garnish with the toasted flaked almonds.

Rex Fairbrother's working conditions are rather less clinical. He runs the free-range pig enterprise based at Hollowtree. This former farm was acquired by Brookfield in the 1960s, and the house sold for flats. In 2015, Rex and his brother Toby obtained the rental of one of the remaining buildings and some land. Initially this was for their geese operation, subsequently for Scruff gin (indoors) and the pigs (outdoors). And if there is one thing Rex has become familiar with as a result, it is mud.

As the late afternoon light fades, a large flock of rooks flies overhead; a thousand bomber raid making purposeful progress southwards. They are too distant for Rex to make out the subtle signs which distinguish them from the similar carrion crow. But he can be confident in his identification. Bert has often told him: 'If you see one rook, him's a crow. And if you see a lot of crows, them's rooks.'

Rex envies their power of flight, as his wellied feet slurp through the chocolate-coloured clag. A hard frost means a respite from mud, but then the water in the drinking troughs turns to ice, and the pipes supplying them freeze solid. At least today Rex has been saved a relentless round of ice breaking and topping up. His large, confident hands were once ideal for plucking a line-out ball from the air, until his role as a professional rugby player was cut short by a neck injury. Now the orange twine around a straw bale bites into his fingers. Baler twine is to farming what duct tape is to engineering – the universal fastener (although farmers use plenty of duct tape too). It has a thousand and one agricultural uses, one of the most frequent being fence or gate repairs. Belts, shoelaces, dog leads, loo roll holders . . . It can even be used to start fires.

Before the light goes completely, Rex has some arks to straw down. When you hear 'ark', banish from your mind any picture of a flood-survival vessel measured in cubits. His pig arks are curved-roofed, made of corrugated metal, with a semi-circular cross section; like a scaled-down version of wartime Nissen huts. A bit of fresh, clean straw to bed down on will keep his charges cosy tonight. Rex delves into his jacket, fumbling to retrieve his pocket knife. His chilled fingers can barely get a purchase on the thin strip of blade edging the scratched wooden handle, but with an effort he prises it open and cuts the cords on the bale. This is his last job of the day, and he consoles himself with the prospect of a rib-sticking meal later. Bert is cooking a speciality of his deceased wife Freda. He has promised there will be plenty to share, and there could be nothing better after a day under the bleak December skies.

STEAK AND KIDNEY PIE
Serves 4–6

3 tbsp plain flour
750g chuck steak, trimmed and cut into 3–4cm chunks
3 tbsp vegetable oil
2 lambs' kidneys
2 onions, peeled and sliced
2 garlic cloves, peeled and chopped
150ml red wine
500ml beef stock
2 tsp Worcestershire sauce
1 bay leaf
2 thyme sprigs
salt and black pepper

Pastry
400g plain flour, plus extra for rolling
pinch of salt
250g cold butter, diced
2 large eggs

Preheat the oven to 150°C/Fan 130°C/Gas 2. Put the flour in
a bowl and season it with salt and pepper. Add the cubes of
steak and toss well, so it is all lightly coated in flour. Heat 2
tablespoons of the oil in a flameproof casserole dish and brown
the meat in batches, then set it aside. Remove the white cores
from the kidneys, then cut them into quarters. Brown the
kidneys and set them aside with the steak.

Add the remaining oil to the dish, add the onions and cook until softened. Add the garlic and fry for another minute or so. Put the steak and kidney back into the dish and pour in the wine. Bring to the boil, stirring well to lift any crispy bits from the bottom of the dish. Pour in the stock, then add the Worcestershire sauce and herbs. Season with salt and pepper. Bring back to the boil, then put a lid on the dish and transfer to the oven for 2 hours. Remove and leave to cool completely.

Meanwhile, make the pastry. Put the flour, salt and butter in a food processor and pulse until the mixture has the texture of breadcrumbs. Beat one of the eggs with 2 tablespoons of cold water, add this to the food processor and pulse until everything starts to come together. Remove the dough and shape it into a ball with your hands, then divide it into about two-thirds and one-third. Preheat the oven to 200°C/Fan 180°C/Gas 6.

Roll out the larger portion of pastry on a floured work surface and place it in a pie dish – you'll need one with a capacity of about 1.2 litres – then pile in the filling. Beat the remaining egg and use some to brush the edges of the pastry. Roll out the smaller piece of pastry and place it over the filling, crimping the edges neatly to seal. Cut a small hole in the top to release steam and brush the pastry with the rest of the beaten egg. Bake for 35–40 minutes until the pastry is crisp and golden. Serve hot with some green vegetables.

'Cor, put the heater on, can't you?'

'It is on.'

For the Grundys, early December means all hands on deck, as the turkeys must be prepared in time for Christmas deliveries. The fate of their birds sounds like a sentence passed down by a medieval court: killed, plucked, hung, drawn and dressed. This is a very hands-on process. At the pole barn in Grundy's Field, Eddie plays Lord High Executioner.

Ed has joined his mother in the shed nearby, where an ancient paraffin heater is fighting a losing battle with the cold and damp. Clarrie is in charge of plucking duties.

Ed settles down on a battered kitchen chair.

'How are the sheep, Edward?'

'Yeah, fine.'

Ed has arrived straight from feeding his Texels. Each ewe has had an ultrasound scan, so he knows how many lambs they are carrying, and he has split them into groups so they can get the appropriate rations. Singles are fine, twins are better, but he hopes not to have too many triplets; there can be complications with the birth.

Ed picks up a freshly killed turkey. 'Better get on with it, then.'

Behind the Scenes
The turkeys must be plucked while they are still warm, and the action of pulling feathers from the skin makes a very specific noise. In *The Archers* studio, the sound effects person recreates it by tugging out tufts from a piece of old carpet.

'Two more, Dad.'

'Thanks, son. Stick 'em in the store, can you?'

The plucked turkeys will hang in the 'cold store' – actually an old lorry container – for ten days, so the flavour develops and the meat tenderises. Then the kitchen at Grange Farm becomes a Tarantino-esque location for a day, when the turkeys' innards are removed – the 'drawing' – and the edible bits popped into plastic bags, for those customers who like to make giblet gravy. Finally, they are boxed up nicely for delivery.

For years, the Grundys had a strong grip on the local market for fresh, free-range Christmas poultry. Why queue at a butcher in Borchester, when you could have your bird raised and delivered less than a mile from your front door? Then, in 2015, the Fairbrothers arrived, with a desire to farm, and an idea that geese were an affordable way in. Joe and Eddie were outraged at these young pretenders muscling in on their patch, especially when plausible Toby managed to persuade many locals to try a seasonal goose for a change.

As Christmas approached, many Grundy turkeys remained unsold. But things were not running smoothly in the Fairbrother camp either. Rex and Toby had grossly underestimated the work involved in preparing their geese for sale. Toby managed to recruit Clarrie's experienced hands to help them, in exchange for a joint mass sell-off of Fairbrother and Grundy birds at the Christmas food market in Felpersham. Toby was so successful in his role as a Victorian trader that the Grundys were left with no turkey for themselves – so he gave them a goose instead! Joe said he would rather starve than eat a Fairbrother bird, but strangely enough he managed to force some down on the day.

For most of us, leftover turkey does not mean unsold stock, but rather the daunting remnants of Christmas dinner. This recipe puts them to good use.

CURRIED TURKEY SOUP
Serves 4

2 tbsp olive oil
2 onions, peeled and sliced into thin wedges
1 carrot, peeled and diced
2 celery sticks, diced
1 red pepper, deseeded and diced
1 green pepper, deseeded and diced
100g butternut squash, peeled and diced
4 garlic cloves, peeled and finely chopped

DECEMBER

10g fresh root ginger, grated
1 red chilli, finely chopped
1 bay leaf
1 tbsp mild curry powder
½ tsp cayenne pepper (optional)
25g basmati rice, unrinsed
1 litre turkey or chicken stock
300g leftover cooked turkey, diced
coriander leaves, roughly chopped
salt and black pepper

To serve
3 tbsp flaked almonds, lightly toasted
thick plain yoghurt
mango chutney
warm naan bread (optional)

Heat the olive oil in a large saucepan. Add the onions, carrot and celery and sauté over a high heat, stirring regularly, for about 10 minutes. When the vegetables are starting to brown around the edges, add the peppers, squash, garlic, ginger and chilli. Cook for another 5 minutes, then add the bay leaf, curry powder and cayenne, if using. Stir to combine.

Stir in the basmati rice, then pour over the stock. Season with salt and pepper and bring to the boil. Turn down the heat and cook, uncovered, until the rice and the vegetables are just tender. Taste for seasoning and adjust as necessary.

Add the diced turkey and the coriander leaves and heat through for another couple of minutes.

Serve in bowls and sprinkle with the flaked almonds. Put the yoghurt and mango chutney on the table so everyone can help themselves and swirl some into their bowl. You could also serve with naan bread if you like.

In December, there is very little to do on the arable crops. The ground is usually too wet to sustain tractor movements, or too frost-hard to work. At Home Farm Adam can spend some time snug in his well-insulated eco-office, making plans for the coming months. But it is still a busy time for livestock farmers, whether they have animals out in the fields, or housed for the winter.

Brookfield's dairy herd is now indoors. But although they must be fed, watered and generally cared for, by Christmas at least the twice-daily task of milking will reduce to nothing. This is because in 2016 Brookfield made a wholesale move to spring calving. UK dairy farmers have led a precarious life for many years. The price paid for their milk has oscillated wildly, often due to world market forces. And costs – including feed – have steadily risen. Pip, David and Ruth cannot do much about global overproduction, Russian import bans or the level of demand from China. So they have concentrated on their costs. The cheapest way to feed a cow is on grass, especially grass which the cow grazes for herself in the field. With its temperate climate and plenty of rain, Britain is ideally placed to grow the green stuff, at least from March to October. So now the Brookfield cows are 'dried off' and will not produce any milk for a couple of months.

Most of the cows and heifers are pregnant. Those that are not 'in calf' will be culled. Strictly speaking, this term doesn't simply mean killed. It applies to any animal that leaves the herd, for whatever reason and regardless of where they finish up. In this case though, they are destined initially for Borchester Market and then for the abattoir, so they will go early in the month, before those establishments close for the festive season.

Kate Madikane (née Aldridge), purveyor of New Age therapies at Spiritual Home, claims not to be much bothered about Christmas – although woe betide any family member who takes her at her word and fails to cough up a present. Kate thinks that the shortest day, 21 December, is a much more authentic festival. She first held a winter solstice party in 1998, at the age of twenty-one. The family feared that they would be forced into performing pagan rituals. Brian in particular had visions of naked dancing around a bonfire. But in the end, it was a rather charming affair.

◇◇◇◇◇◇◇◇◇◇◇◇◇◇◇◇◇◇◇◇◇◇◇◇◇◇◇◇◇◇◇◇◇◇◇◇◇◇◇

Ambridge International

USA

◇◇◇◇◇◇◇◇◇◇◇◇◇◇◇◇◇◇◇◇◇◇◇◇◇◇◇◇◇◇◇◇◇◇◇◇◇◇◇

Although Kate specialises in outraging her parents, her sister Alice has her moments, too. When she and Chris Carter got together at a music festival in 2008, the delight of his parents was matched only by the dismay of hers. Despite their different backgrounds, the relationship survived the separation when Alice went to university, and in 2010 they took a road trip in the USA.

On their return, they stunned everyone by announcing that Chris had proposed at the Grand Canyon, and they had married at the Crystal Heart Chapel, Las Vegas. Jennifer was devastated that her ambitious daughter had hitched herself to the son of a pigman – especially as it meant that Jennifer was now related to the Horrobin family! Brian did his best to console her. For the sake of their sanity, he said, they should consider this Alice's 'starter marriage'.

AMERICAN-STYLE CHOPPED SALAD
Serves 4

1 romaine lettuce heart, finely shredded
50g rocket, roughly chopped
½ cucumber, deseeded and diced
4 medium tomatoes, deseeded and diced
100g radishes, sliced into rounds
3 celery sticks, diced
6 spring onions, sliced into thin rounds
½ punnet of mustard cress
2 tarragon sprigs, finely chopped
small bunch of parsley, finely chopped
a few basil leaves, roughly torn
2 cooked chicken breasts, diced
1 avocado, peeled and diced
juice of ½ lime

Dressing
3 tbsp olive oil
2 tsp cider vinegar
¼ tsp honey
1 tsp Dijon mustard
½ garlic clove, crushed
1 tbsp warm water
salt and black pepper

Put all the salad vegetables and herbs into a large salad bowl and add the diced chicken. Toss the avocado in the lime juice and add this as well. Fold everything together gently – you don't want to bruise the avocado too much.

For the dressing, whisk the oil, vinegar, honey and mustard together, then stir in the garlic. Season with salt and pepper. Taste and adjust the acidity as necessary, then add the warm water to thin the dressing.

Pour the salad dressing over the salad just before serving and toss. Make sure you do this at the last minute so the vegetables don't go soggy. Serve immediately.

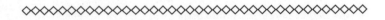

'Where did you grow up, Rosie?'

'Borsetshire. A little village called Ambridge.'

'And what were your Christmases like?'

Rosie Ruth Grace Archer thought back to her childhood days at Brookfield Farm.

'Warm.'

The general impression in Rosie's mind resolves itself into a clear memory. Sitting at the table in the Aga-cheered kitchen, making paper chains or glitter-strewn cards, the aroma of some delicious treat tantalising her nostrils. Great-Gran Jill was by then well into her eighties, but she could still conjure up a three-course meal for a dozen people, apparently without effort. And if the mischievous twinkle ever left her eyes while she did so, then Rosie was not around to see it.

In the sitting room, the fire blazed, its dancing flames kaleidoscoped a hundred times by the baubles adorning the Christmas tree. It was so tall that the angel at its tip had to duck her head, looking down benevolently as Mum and Uncle Ben laughed with her. She was never short of playmates, even if her charming and mercurial father Toby wasn't always on hand. So many schemes, so many dreams . . . But when he was there, she never doubted that he loved his little 'Rose Petal' in his own special way.

Every family has its own Christmas traditions, a patch-work of folk custom, religious ritual, new adoptions and unspoken expectations. For Rosie, no Christmas was complete without at least one visit to Deck the Hall. Growing up, she thought it was perfectly normal to have a great-aunt who commanded a stately home. After all, Elsa and Anna lived in a snow-clad castle. Why would Auntie Lily and Uncle Freddie not live in a grand mansion? Lower Loxley was her own fantasy land, and it was never better than at Christmas time.

The centrepiece was always the ice rink. Rosie cannot remember how old she was when she took her first tenta-tive steps onto that slippery surface. But she can certainly remember the comforting security of her grandad's hand. And when they left the ice, hearts pumping and cheeks burnished by the chill air, it was time to visit the food stalls. A ring of alpine huts, each a treasure trove of wildly exotic delights. Gingerbread hearts, tingling with spice. Candied almonds, their scent intoxicating as incense. A bratwurst as long as her arm, dwarfing the bread roll on which it was precariously perched. And the hot chocolate. Oh, the hot chocolate . . . Rich as a beanstalk giant, warm as a mother's heart, topped with an Eiger of whipped cream.

Rosie smiles with a sudden realisation. Grandad David usually chose another drink, fruit-red and steaming, served in its own quirky china mug. At the time, she thought it was just the hot blackcurrant squash she would sometimes have when she got home from school, and she could never understand why she wasn't allowed a sip. Of course, she knows now what it was, and why it was such a perfect grown-up accompaniment to a starry December night.

MULLED WINE
Serves 8–10

175g caster sugar
2 bottles of red wine
1 lemon, studded with 6 cloves
2.5cm piece of fresh root ginger
1 cinnamon stick
juice of 2 lemons
thinly pared zest of 1 orange

Put the sugar in a pan with 375ml of water and stir over a low heat until the sugar has dissolved. Add the wine and remaining ingredients and heat gently until steaming. Don't let it boil.

Remove the pan from the heat, cover with a lid and allow to stand for 10 minutes. Remove the lemon and cloves, ginger and cinnamon stick, but leave the orange zest to float in the wine. Pour into a warmed punch bowl if you have one or serve from the pan.

CHAPTER FIVE
January

'Ah'm no' likely to forget the date, big man. It's the same every year.'

'I just wanted to check, that's all.'

'Ah'll be there, Kenton, niver ye mind.'

Jack McCreary is always known as Jazzer, except to his ma – and the police. Oh yes, in his younger days Jazzer brushed up against Borsetshire Constabulary quite frequently. For a while he led schoolmate Ed Grundy into numerous petty crimes, including joyriding and burglary. Both were fortunate to put that life behind them and have become (fairly) respectable members of society.

Now Jazzer holds down two jobs; doing an early morning milk delivery and being Adam's right-hand man on the aquaponics setup at Home Farm. Jazzer was testing one of the fish tanks when Kenton rang him about Burns Night. As usual, The Bull is planning the full works for 25 January. It is a good money-spinner in a traditionally pockets-empty month, when punters are watching their waistlines and resting their livers. Burns Night suppers can bring out the part-time Scot in almost anyone, but Jazzer is the real deal, as Glasgow-built as a Clyde steamer. Kenton has booked him and his bagpipes – part musical instrument, part weapon of war – for one of the essential moments of the night: piping in the haggis.

'Ha' ye got someone for the "Address tae the Haggis", yet?'

Kenton clears this throat. 'I'm working on it.'

'Working on it?'

'I did ask Chris Carter, but he didn't fancy it.'

'Well, that's whit ye should be daeing, not chasing me.'

'All right, all right. I'll sort it.'

While Kenton is wondering who might take on Robert Burns' eight-verse Scots dialect poem, his mother Jill is tipping a cascade of sugar into a preserving pan. In 2003, the Ambridge Flower and Produce Show had an 'unusual marmalade' class. Jill won second prize with her lemon and quince recipe, but the judges looked less kindly on her other offerings: lemon and ginger; lime and passion fruit; brandy; onion. Bert Fry's wife Freda took the top prize (one of many over the years) with a ginger version. Today Jill is sticking to a classic recipe, during the very short Seville orange season. Those bittersweet globes of sunshine are ideal for the task.

SEVILLE ORANGE MARMALADE
Makes 8–10 jars

1.5kg Seville oranges
2 unwaxed lemons
1.5kg granulated sugar
knob of butter

Wash the oranges and lemons well, then cut them in half and squeeze out the juice into a bowl. Remove the pips as you go and set them aside.

Cut the orange and lemon halves into thin strips with a sharp knife or use a food processor. Put the strips of peel and any pulp in a large heavy-based pan. Wrap the pips in a piece of muslin, tie it securely and add it to the pan.

Pour 3.5 litres of water into the pan, bring it to the boil and cook gently until the peel is soft and the water is reduced by about half. This will take about 2 hours.

Take the pan off the heat and remove the bag of pips, squeezing it to extract any juice. Add the sugar and stir until it has all dissolved, then put the pan back over the heat. Place a couple of saucers in the freezer for testing the set of the marmalade.

Bring the marmalade to the boil and boil rapidly for 10–15 minutes. Start testing after 10 minutes – you don't want to overboil it. Put a teaspoonful of marmalade on one of the cold saucers. If it wrinkles when you push it with your finger, it's ready. If not, continue to boil for a few more minutes, then test again.

When the setting point has been reached, take the pan off the heat. Stir in a knob of butter to disperse any scum. Leave to cool for a few minutes, then pour the marmalade into warm sterilised jars – take care, it will still be extremely hot. Cover and store in a cool dark place. Marmalade keeps well for months.

JANUARY

As she stirs the sugar into the steaming orange mixture,
Jill thinks of the time her husband Phil very nearly put
his foot in it. He was about to express a preference for
the marmalade made by Ruth's mother Heather, but he
realised just in time on which side his bread was buttered.
Smiling, Jill resolves to take a jar to Phil's sister Christine
when she next visits her sheltered flat. They often book a
lunch in the home itself. The food at The Laurels isn't bad,
she thinks. For an institution . . .

TANGY TREACLE TART
Serves 6

2 eggs, beaten
450g golden syrup
grated zest of 1 unwaxed
  lemon
125g brown breadcrumbs

Pastry
250g plain flour, plus extra
  for rolling
pinch of salt
150g cold butter, diced
1 large egg, beaten

First make the pastry. Put the flour, salt and butter in a food processor and pulse until the mixture resembles breadcrumbs. Add the beaten egg and pulse again until the mixture starts to come together. Turn it out into a bowl and shape it into a round.

Put the pastry on a floured surface and roll it out until it is about the thickness of a pound coin. Line a 23cm tart tin and trim the pastry to fit – keep the trimmings and any other bits of pastry to make the lattice top. Put the pastry case in the fridge to chill for about 30 minutes.

For the filling, beat the eggs in a bowl, then add the syrup, lemon zest and breadcrumbs. Mix until everything is well combined.

Preheat the oven to 200°C/Fan 180°C/Gas 6. Prick the pastry base, then pour in the filling. Roll out the pastry trimmings and cut them into strips. Place these over the tart to create a lattice effect, pressing them down lightly at the edges.

Bake the tart for about 30 minutes until set and golden brown. Allow to cool slightly before serving with some cream or ice cream.

The farming side of Jill's family mainly have livestock on their mind, and it is a lot of livestock. Out in the fields are sheep and some Hereford youngstock. Indoors, they have the Hereford suckler cows and calves; fattening Hereford youngstock, which are near to slaughter; the dairy herd, which are by now all dried off; and an increasing number of ewes. There are a lot of bellies to fill, so the yard and the buildings around it become a major focus of activity.

Out in Coombebell, Josh takes hay and sheep pellets – concentrated feed – to the ewes.

Behind the Scenes
In *The Archers* studio, dry dog food stands in for the various concentrated feeds – dairy nuts, sheep pellets, pignuts – and a metal bucket for the trough they are poured into.

As Josh dumps a bale of hay into the feeder, he wonders what on earth possessed him to take on the challenge of Dry January. Ironically, he only agreed to do it because he was drunk on New Year's Eve and got into a silly escalating barney with Rex, his partner in the egg business. But once issued, the challenge was impossible to refuse without losing face. Josh still has a young man's brittle ego and keenly feels any slight to his 'rep' (utation). All the same, he thinks, what a stupid month to give up booze! The first of February will be measured in pints and shots, but until then he has to make do with fizzy drinks and alcohol-free concoctions dreamed up by his uncle Kenton.

POMEGRANATE AND LIME SPARKLE

pomegranate juice
sparkling water
freshly squeezed lime juice
honey
pomegranate seeds
twist of lime
ice (optional)

Mix equal parts of pomegranate juice and sparkling water in a large glass. Add freshly squeezed lime juice to taste and stir in a spoonful of honey.

Add a few pomegranate seeds and a twist of lime and serve with or without ice.

Back in the yard, the dairy cows are helping themselves. Their heads poke through the gaps in a metal feed barrier, keenly scoffing the silage which earlier today David had spread on the concrete with a piece of kit called a tele-handler. So what is silage? As dear departed Nigel Pargetter once asked, 'Is that the smelly stuff?' The brief answer (long-suffering Phil Archer often used to give Nigel pretty brief answers) is 'fermented grass'. Just as sauerkraut is a way of preserving cabbage by a process of fermentation, silaging is a method of preserving large amounts of grass, so it can be fed to livestock through the winter. Aside from its nutritional value, it has the great advantage to the farmer that it is literally home-grown and home-made, so cheaper than any bought-in feed.

Until about 1970, by far the most popular method of turning British grass into winter fodder was haymaking. Hay is dried grass. That sounds simple but, as we will see, haymaking is critically dependent on the weather being co-operative at the time of cutting and immediately afterwards. There are far fewer worries with silage, which has much more leeway over its moisture content. You cut and chop your grass, squash the air out of it, and keep it airtight somehow, so the anaerobic fermentation process can happen. The silage that the Brookfield cows are chomping on is made in the traditional way, in a clamp – literally a pile. A massive rectangular pile covered in plastic sheeting and weighed down with old tyres.

Although silage is more reliable to make than hay, it still needs grass. This is why the shirts-off-swim-in-the-fountains-I-can't-believe-it's-not-Athens summer of 2018 was such bad news for Brookfield, and for almost all British livestock farmers. The torrid weather and lack of rain meant there was much less grass for the cows to graze, so Brookfield had to start on their winter food supplies earlier

than usual. As the months drew on, their clamp was looking worryingly scanty, so David, Ruth, Pip and Josh had to
do some nifty sideways thinking to get enough nutrition
into their beasts.

One answer was to buy in straw – although seeing that
David was desperate, the merchant struck a fairly high
price for it. Straw is simply the stalks of cereal plants,
like wheat and barley. It's more usually used for bedding
(indeed, all Brookfield's indoor cattle are housed on straw).
But as a feed it does have some value. It is high in fibre,
although short on flavour and some nutrients. They mixed
it with the silage they had, plus molasses for protein and
a mineral supplement, and fed that to the dairy herd. The
beef cattle had a rather more unusual diet, including broken biscuits and bakery waste, which Josh had somehow
procured. It wasn't ideal, and a lot more costly than usual.
But by adding essential nutritional extras, they kept their
animals healthy through the winter.

'Come on . . . you'd be great at it.'

For a man with a hammer in his hand, Chris Carter
looks remarkably bashful.

'No, Jolene. I told Kenton . . .' With strong but precise
strokes, he fine-tunes a glowing horseshoe on the anvil.
'Public speaking . . . it's not my thing.'

'What do you mean? You were great as Harrison's best
man.'

'That was a nightmare!'

'You won't have to write anything, though. It's just saying a poem.'

'I'll never remember all those Scottish words.'

'Read it, then. No one'll mind.' Jolene's mid-Atlantic contralto softens to a seductive purr. 'There's a free dinner in it for you.'

Chris looks up. 'And drinks?'

'Don't see why not. Within reason.'

On the road outside, Kirsty Miller is plugging through a freezing drizzle as she cycles home. Her spirits are lifted slightly by the sight of the first snowdrops in the verge, delicate but dauntless, heralds of the still distant spring. A kestrel hovers over the hedgerow. Everyman's hawk, a roadside sentinel keeping station on the wind, scanning the earth for an unwary field vole or wood mouse.

For many people, the fate of the kestrel's prey is a justification for humans eating meat. It is part of nature's pattern. But an increasing number are uneasy carnivores, whether for reasons of personal health, animal rights or the environment. Kirsty Miller has been following a 'flexitarian' diet for some time, eating only a limited amount of meat reared to high-welfare standards wherever possible. Her environmental conscience has led to some spectacular clashes with (as she sees it) uncaring capitalist despoilers of the earth, especially Brian Aldridge and Justin Elliott. The

IPCC's warnings that we all need to drastically reduce our meat consumption to combat climate change strengthened her resolve. So, this month, she is attempting to avoid all meat, fish and dairy products.

VEGAN BAKE
Serves 4

Roast vegetables
½ red cabbage, cut into wedges
½ cauliflower, broken into florets
¼ celeriac, cut into thin wedges
2 red onions, peeled and cut into wedges
1 red pepper, deseeded and cut into thick strips
2 tbsp olive oil
2–3 cooked beetroots, cut into wedges
salt and black pepper

Sauce
1 tbsp olive oil
1 onion, peeled and finely chopped
10g fresh root ginger, grated
4 garlic cloves, peeled and finely chopped
1 tsp mustard seeds
1 tsp cumin seeds
1 tsp coriander seeds, lightly crushed
1 tsp ground cardamom
½ tsp nigella seeds

½ tsp ground cardamom
½ tsp ground turmeric
400g can of chickpeas, drained
200g canned tomatoes

Topping
50g fresh breadcrumbs
4 tbsp finely chopped coriander stems
zest of 1 lime
olive oil

To serve
coriander leaves
lime wedges

Preheat the oven to 200°C/Fan 180°C/Gas 6.

Arrange the cabbage, cauliflower, celeriac, red onions and
red pepper over the base of a large oven dish or roasting tin.
Season with salt and pepper and drizzle with olive oil. Roast in
the oven for 20 minutes, then add the cooked beetroots and
roast for 10 minutes longer.

While the vegetables are roasting, make the sauce. Heat
the oil in a saucepan and add the onion. Cook until soft and
translucent, then add the ginger, garlic and spices. Cook for
another 2–3 minutes, then add the chickpeas, tomatoes and
200ml of water. Bring to the boil and simmer for 5 minutes.

Remove the vegetables from the oven and pour the chickpeas and their sauce over them. Mix together the breadcrumbs with plenty of seasoning, the coriander and lime zest and sprinkle over the contents of the tin or dish. Drizzle with a little more olive oil.

Bake for another 10–15 minutes until the breadcrumbs are crisp and golden brown. Sprinkle with coriander leaves and serve with lime wedges.

JANUARY

◇◇

Ambridge International

MEXICO

◇◇

'I thought I might make a chilli tonight, Neil.'

A slow smile spreads over Neil's face.

'Sounds lovely.' He kisses Susan warmly and heads off to work with a jaunty air.

The 'less meat' message has not really reached Ambridge View. And you could hardly expect it to, given that Neil Carter has spent a lifetime rearing pigs and Susan works on a farm that sells beef and sausages. Although Susan's daughter eventually married Ed Grundy, Emma had initially chosen his brother Will. They were married in 2004 and honeymooned in Mexico. As part of his pay as a gamekeeper, Will had a tied cottage – actually a decent-sized three-bedroom house. Infused with the Latin spirit, and with a glimmer of her mother's desire to edge up the social ladder, on their return Emma gave the place the Spanish name Casa Nueva ('new home'). But the marriage was built on sands as light as the beaches of Cancún. Sleeping with the best man on your hen night is never a recommended course of action for the bride-to-be. Divorce came in 2006.

After years in gloomy isolation, Will eventually found

true love with Nic, of blessed memory. When he carried
the new Mrs Grundy over the threshold, she was
delighted, but asked if he would mind changing the name
of the house. Immediately grasping the unspoken association with Emma, Will quickly dubbed it Greenwood
Cottage. The final trace of his blighted first marriage was
erased – at least externally.

But perhaps Emma's Latin adventure lives on in a way
she does not realise, and in fact would shudder to contem-
plate. Some time later, it became apparent that the classic
Tex-Mex dish of chilli con carne was playing an important
role in Susan and Neil's marital life. Enjoyment in the
kitchen seemed to lead to enjoyment in the bedroom –
so much so that some *Archers* listeners renamed the dish
'chilli con carnal'. There may be some genuine physiolog-
ical basis for this. A substance in chilli peppers stimulates
nerve endings on the tongue, releasing adrenaline, which
increases the heart rate and produces endorphins. And
both chilli peppers and garlic contain allicin, which can
be good for blood circulation – to where, you can deduce
yourself, Watson. In any case, Susan and Neil don't give a
monkey's about the science. They know what works for
them, and you can't argue with that.

CHILLI CON CARNE
Serves 4

2 tbsp olive oil
1 large onion, peeled and finely diced
1 red pepper, deseeded and diced
1 green pepper, deseeded and diced
400g minced beef
200g minced pork
4 garlic cloves, peeled and finely chopped
2–3 tsp chipotle paste
2 tbsp finely chopped coriander stems
1 tbsp dried oregano
1 tbsp ground cumin
1 tsp cinnamon
200ml milk
400g can of tomatoes
2 x 400g cans of red kidney beans, drained
200ml beef stock or water
2 bay leaves
salt and black pepper

To serve
cooked long grain rice
grated cheese
leaves from a small bunch of coriander
soured cream
lime wedges

Heat the olive oil in a large flameproof casserole dish. Add the onion and peppers and cook over a very low heat until the onion is soft and translucent. Turn the heat up high and add the meat. Sear it quickly on all sides until well browned, then turn the heat down again.

Add the garlic and chipotle paste and stir them into the meat. Cook for a couple of minutes, then add the coriander stems, dried oregano and spices. Stir to combine, then pour over the milk, canned tomatoes, kidney beans and stock. Tuck in the bay leaves and season with salt and pepper.

Bring to the boil, then cover and turn down the heat. Leave to simmer for an hour, checking regularly to make sure the chilli isn't catching on the bottom of the pan. Remove the lid and continue to cook until it is well reduced and thick. Serve with rice and the garnishes.

Some home-made walnut bread is ideal to chase the final tasty morsels round the bowl. Assuming that by the end of the meal you are not too distracted, that is.

WHOLEMEAL WALNUT LOAF

1 tsp quick-acting dried yeast
1 tsp sugar
500g wholemeal flour, plus extra for dusting
1 tsp salt
about 350ml tepid water
3 tbsp olive oil, plus extra for greasing
150g walnuts, chopped

Put the yeast, sugar, flour and salt into a large bowl and mix well. Stir in the water, then the olive oil and mix until everything comes together into a soft dough.

Turn the dough out onto a floured work surface and knead well until smooth. Cover the bowl with a damp tea towel or cling film and leave it in a warm place for an hour or so, until doubled in size. Grease a 900g loaf tin with oil.

Knead the dough again, then add the walnuts and continue kneading to incorporate them into the dough. Put the dough into the loaf tin, cover and leave to rise again. Preheat the oven to 220°C/Fan 200°C/Gas 7.

Bake the loaf for 45 minutes or until the base feels hollow when tapped. Turn the loaf out of the tin and leave it to cool on a wire rack.

It is not until the end of the month that work may be able to restart on the arable crops, so apart from what state Jazzer will be in on 26 January, Adam's main concern right now is his animals. At Home Farm, the deer are outdoors. And for much of the month so are the sheep, making their new year's resolutions ('eat grass', 'try to escape', 'eat more grass'). Some of them are grazing the Italian ryegrass, which Adam planted beneath the maize last year. Not only has it helped to protect the soil, but it is also providing food at this lean time. And the luckiest sheep have the treat of being let loose on some of the herbal leys.

These are one of Adam's big guns in the battle to restore the health of Home Farm's soil. 'Ley' means a human-made pasture, and that is exactly what these are. Adam has sown a cheerful chaos of plant species, many with fabulous antique names like bird's-foot trefoil, rib-grass plantain and meadow fescue. The mixture can include over a dozen species, but usually involves a combination of grasses, herbs and legumes. Like Tom's clover, many of them fix (absorb) nitrogen from the atmosphere, and so fertilise the soil when they are ploughed back in, usually after about four years.

The unkempt, natural look of a herbal ley in full flower is a striking contrast to the uniform vistas which dominate most British fields. A green gallimaufry of shapes and sizes jostles shoulder to shoulder, like fans on match day. Dainty white clover – like land-bound sea anemones – tut censoriously at the shameless baby blue of the chicory flower, while the 'holy hay' of sainfoin looks down in pink disdain on both. But the real work is happening out of sight underground, as the deep roots unlock precious nutrients and improve soil structure.

On this January day, there are no flowers, but the sheep greedily nibble their mixed green salad, rich in minerals. Towards the end of the month, the ewes who are due to give birth first will be moved into a shed – not a wooden garden-type thing, but one of those large pitch-roofed, steel-sided affairs that you see on farms all over the country. How does Adam know which are going to lamb first? By the magic of raddle, of course, which he was careful to employ when the rams were doing their job back in the autumn. He will put them in two distinct areas, separated by metal hurdles, depending on how many lambs they are carrying – just like Ed Grundy did, although on a smaller scale, last month.

'Good Lord, that's loud!'

'What?!'

'I said . . . never mind.'

Alan Franks gives up trying to make conversation and joins in with the rest of the diners, clapping to the march time of 'Scotland the Brave'. Smiling Jolene parades among the tables, brandishing a silver salver on which sits the guest of honour: a plump brown haggis. Behind her walks Jazzer in full Highland dress, his pipes set to 'obliterate'.

Jolene sets the salver down on the top table and the music ends with a drone's dying fall. Wondering how he ever got talked into this, Chris Carter stands in the sudden silence, lifts the ceremonial dagger and takes a deep breath.

'Fair fa' your honest, sonsie face,
Great chieftain o' the puddin'-race!
Aboon them a' ye tak your place . . .'

HAGGIS WITH NEEPS AND TATTIES
Serves 4

1 haggis
1kg floury potatoes, peeled and cut into chunks
2 tbsp olive oil, dripping or lard
1 large swede (neeps), peeled and diced
50g butter, plus extra for dotting over the potatoes
salt and white pepper

Preheat the oven to 180°C/Fan 160°C/Gas 4.

Remove the outer packaging from the haggis and put it in an ovenproof dish. Add a couple of centimetres of water to the dish and cover tightly with foil. Bake at the bottom of the oven for 75 minutes for a haggis weighing 500g, or 90 minutes for a larger one.

Bring a large pan of water to the boil and add plenty of salt and the potatoes. Bring to the boil and boil for 5 minutes, then drain and roughly break up – they don't need to be mashed, but they should be rough around the edges and broken up a bit.

Heat the olive oil, dripping or lard in a large roasting tin. Add the potatoes, stir them around a little to coat them in the fat, then squash them together – there shouldn't be too many gaps. Put the potatoes in the oven at the point when the haggis still needs an hour to cook. Roast for an hour, shaking or turning them over occasionally.

While the haggis and potatoes are in the oven, cook the swede in plenty of boiling water until tender. Drain and tip it back into the pan to dry out a little, then add the 50g of butter and plenty of salt and white pepper. Mash coarsely – again, the swede should be crushed rather than worked into a smooth purée or mash.

Remove the haggis and potatoes from the oven. Break the haggis open (it will burst as soon as you put a knife to it, so be careful) and spoon it out into a warm serving dish. Dot butter over the potatoes and let it melt over them and serve with the haggis and the swede.

CHAPTER SIX

February

Nature's multiple personality disorder is seldom more evident than in February. The shortest month can sometimes seem like the longest, as we grind day-to-day through grey or storm or snow or flood. The month was sometimes known as February Fill Dyke for good reason. But at the same time, the earth is awakening, determinedly edging forward into rebirth and regrowth. And the reason for this? The sun. By the 21st, the winter solstice is two months behind us, and the sun – whether you can see the blessed thing or not – rises an hour earlier and sets an hour and a half later. It may not seem like it, as we tighten our scarves and shudder in the blast of a bitter north-easterly, but we are almost a third of the way to Midsummer Day.

The lengthening days awake the arable crops which, yawning and stretching, demand feeding. Not as we do with a bowl of muesli or a bacon roll, but with the magic trio known to farmers as NPK. Those are the chemical symbols for nitrogen, phosphorous and potassium, the three major nutrients that plants need to thrive. Unfortunately, the pests and crop diseases are also starting to flex their muscles. To attend to all of these, Adam will be hoping for some kind days, so he can get out on the Home Farm and Berrow Estate land with the sprayer. And if the ground is dry enough, he will take the deliciously named crumble roller to prepare the fields where he is planning to sow spring crops.

Entry on the Ambridge website:

Don't give a toss this Pancake Day! Come to The Bull and enjoy our freshly prepared sweet and savoury pancakes. Select from our delicious filling combinations, including vegetarian options – or go wild and create your own!

———

And the fun doesn't stop there. Enter our famous Pancake Derby. Adult, teen and child races with attractive prizes on offer. Or if you'd rather just watch, that's fine too. Everyone welcome!

———

Pancakes available from 6 p.m., races start at 6.30.

———

The Bull is a Free House, serving Shires and other fine ales. Try our Scruff gin, made locally here in Ambridge.

PANCAKES
Makes about 12

Batter	Toppings	French-style
125g plain flour	lemon wedges,	*Suzette sauce*
pinch of salt	sugar, jam,	4 tbsp sugar
2 eggs, beaten	maple syrup,	50g butter
275ml milk	lemon curd,	juice of 2 oranges
40g butter	chocolate spread	2 tbsp Grand
		Marnier or
		other liqueur

Sift the flour and salt into a mixing bowl, then make a well in the centre. Pour the eggs into the well and whisk to combine them with the flour. Start adding the milk, a little at a time at first, whisking constantly to avoid any lumps forming. Add the rest of the milk to make a smooth batter, then set it aside to rest.

When you're ready to cook, melt the butter in a small pan and tip two-thirds of it into the batter, leaving the rest for cooking the pancakes. Heat a heavy-based frying pan until really hot and brush it with a little melted butter. Pour in a couple of tablespoons of batter, tilting the pan to spread it evenly over the base. Allow it to cook for a minute or so, then lift one edge. If it comes away easily and is brown in patches, the pancake is ready to turn. Flip it over with a palette knife and cook for another minute, then slide it onto a plate and cover to keep it warm. Brush the pan with butter again and continue until you have used up all the batter. (For some reason, the first pancake is sometimes not the best but is still perfectly edible. Cook's perks?)

Serve with a variety of toppings, so everyone can garnish their own pancakes as they wish.

If you want to get a bit more fancy, try a French-style Suzette sauce. Put the sugar in a frying pan and warm it gently until melted. Remove the pan from the heat, add the butter and orange juice and place the pan back on the heat until the butter has melted. Add the liqueur and simmer gently until you have a glossy sauce. Fold your pancakes into triangles and add them to the pan to warm through, then serve at once.

FEBRUARY

In 2019, Adam started to experiment with more unusual spring crops including linseed, also known as flax, and quinoa, also known as 'how do you pronounce that stuff?' Both flaxseed and quinoa have become fashionable in recent years as so-called superfoods, and are sold by Adam's Archer cousins in the shop at Bridge Farm. Pat and Helen have been preaching the gospel of healthy eating for a long time, and if the waves generated by food bloggers and Instagram influencers wash more people up at their door, then they are happy to ride that tide.

However, you are not likely to see their former pigman Jazzer McCreary filling one of the shop's wicker baskets with spirulina and goji berries. An inveterate salad-dodger, Jazzer is deeply suspicious of any food described as 'good for you'. In 2015, made temporarily homeless by the Great Ambridge Flood, he moved in with his employers. He was grateful for their kindness, but it came at a price. Forced by circumstances to dine with them daily, he found himself shovelling down more hearty wholefoods than he had ever imagined existed.

One lunchtime, it finally got too much. Jazzer fled to The Bull, despite the menu being very limited, as Kenton and Jolene limped back into post-flood operation. Other than sandwiches, all they could offer was microwaved steak and kidney pie or cheese pasty. Jazzer had both. He missed out, though, because Helen's three-lentil bake is delicious.

THREE-LENTIL BAKE
Serves 4

2 tbsp olive oil
1 large onion, peeled and finely chopped
1 large carrot, peeled and diced
2 celery sticks, diced
200g butternut squash, peeled and diced
2 garlic cloves, peeled and finely chopped
1 tsp dried sage
1 thyme sprig
100ml red wine
50g uncooked red lentils, well rinsed
500ml vegetable stock
250g cooked mung beans (75g dried, uncooked)
250g cooked puy lentils (75g dried, uncooked)
2 tsp Dijon mustard
salt and black pepper

Crust
50g fresh breadcrumbs
50g Cheddar cheese, grated
handful of basil leaves, shredded

Heat the olive oil in a large flameproof casserole dish. Add
the onion, carrot, celery and butternut squash and cook over
a medium heat, stirring regularly to prevent them catching.
When the vegetables are starting to take on some colour, add

the garlic, sage and thyme and cook for another couple of minutes, then turn up the heat and add the wine. Bring to the boil and leave to bubble for a couple of minutes, then add the red lentils and the stock. Season with salt and pepper.

Bring everything back to the boil, then turn the heat down to a fast simmer, and leave to cook, partially covered, for 25–30 minutes until the vegetables are tender and the lentils have cooked through and started to collapse. The cooking liquid should be well reduced by this stage and will have thickened from the starch in the lentils.

Preheat the oven to 200°C/Fan 180°C/Gas 6. Stir the mung beans, puy lentils and mustard into the dish. Mix the crust ingredients and season with salt and pepper, then sprinkle this over the surface of the lentils. Bake in the oven for about 20 minutes until the crust is bubbling and golden. Serve with a green salad.

The Archers at Brookfield Farm are about to enter the most frantic time of their year. Their pregnant ewes will start to give birth early next month, so in between their other work they have to prepare the lambing shed. The clanging of alloy hurdles reverberates off the steel walls as David and Ruth assemble the various pens.

Behind the Scenes

Like the lambing shed, *The Archers* studio is also separated into different areas. Lambing scenes are recorded in the 'live end', with its hard floor and walls. This area is used for all the more echoey locations, from the Village Hall to (with some extra electronic reverb) Felpersham Cathedral. Or the space can be reduced using hard panels on wheels to represent smaller places such as a bathroom or the cellar at The Bull.

While David and Ruth make a racket, Pip quietly does an inventory check of all the essential supplies. She will top up any shortfall with a trip to Borsetshire Farmers, the only cash-and-carry where a request for a prolapse harness will not get you thrown out. Top tip, by the way: if you ever mislay your prolapse harness, you can fashion an emergency one using, what else, baler twine.

Pip will also be busy checking the state of the grassland with her platemeter. This gizmo was first introduced to Brookfield by cowman Sam Batton, when he was taken on in 2004. Spaghetti Bolognese can still bring back difficult feelings for David. He was cooking it for the kids when Ruth was away 'meeting an old friend'. In reality, she was on her way to a hotel where Sam was waiting. But in the end she could not go through with the affair.

Despite the bad memories, David still manages to eat

'spag bol', and he tolerates the use of the platemeter on the farm. It is so useful that he probably feels he has no choice. The device is rather reminiscent of a metal detector: a vertical shaft with a handle at the top and a circular disc at the bottom – about the size of the generous dinner plates in the Grey Gables restaurant. Pip walks in zigzags, regularly plonking the plate onto the grass (each sample is informally known as a 'plonk'). The meter electronically records the height of the grass, and software in her laptop estimates the total quantity in the field. So Pip will know scientifically when it is best to let cattle graze it, and when they need to move on to a new area.

As soon as the grass is ready, they will start to let the dairy herd out – just during the daytime at first. Because it reduces their reliance on those precious winter feed stocks, for the family this is a moment of relief. But for the cows it is positively joyous. From the still bare branches of a sycamore, a chaffinch looks down, as exuberantly multi-hued as a Mardi Gras dancer. Below, released onto grass after months indoors, the cows spring around like gazelles. To be honest, the effect is more comic than graceful, but it is a delight to watch – while it lasts. They soon recover their dignity, calm down and are grazing placidly. As the humans walk back to the farmhouse, the chaffinch continues its song, quite uniform in pitch but with a characteristic rhythm, like a bowler running up to the wicket and delivering the ball.

◇◇◇◇◇◇◇◇◇◇◇◇◇◇◇◇◇◇◇◇◇◇◇◇◇◇◇◇◇◇◇◇◇◇◇◇◇

Ambridge International

BULGARIA

◇◇◇◇◇◇◇◇◇◇◇◇◇◇◇◇◇◇◇◇◇◇◇◇◇◇◇◇◇◇◇◇◇◇◇◇◇

Ambridge's real cricketers will be at indoor nets tonight, training for the coming season. Driving to the leisure centre in Borchester, Roy Tucker is reflective. The plaintive soundtrack of Radiohead's *OK Computer* on the car stereo has put him in a sombre mood. His thoughts turn, as they often do, to his former partner, Lexi Viktorova. He remembers the first time she made a traditional Bulgarian banitsa for him (imagine Jazzer's emergency cheese pasty but made by the angels). As Roy bit through the crispy filo and tasted the heavenly filling, Lexi explained how on New Year's Eve her mother would put lucky charms into the mixture, one for each member of the family and one for the Virgin Mary. Each person would take a slice and their fortune for the year would be determined by the charm it contained: health, journey, wealth . . . marriage . . . love.

How Roy and Lexi celebrated when the delicacy won first prize at the Flower and Produce Show, relegating Jennifer's frangipane into also-ran status . . . how happy they were, before that flaming surrogacy idea came along . . . how things were never the same afterwards.

When next year's show came round, Lexi was in

Bulgaria. It was their longest separation since they had started seeing each other. When she came back to Ambridge, weeks later, Roy was so excited. He even made a banitsa to welcome her home. But that night it remained untouched, and so did he. Even if he could not admit it to himself, he knew deep in his heart that it was over.

BULGARIAN BANITSA
Serves 4

12 sheets of filo pastry (30 x 40cm)
100g butter, melted

Filling
400g feta cheese
100g Greek yoghurt
1 egg
1 bunch of spring onions, finely chopped
salt and black pepper

Topping
2 eggs, beaten
100ml Greek yoghurt

Preheat the oven to 200°C/Fan 180°C/Gas 6. Line the base of a 23cm round, loose-bottomed cake tin with baking parchment.

Make the filling. Crumble the feta into a bowl as finely as you can, then stir in the yoghurt, egg and spring onions. Season with salt and pepper. The mixture should be thick and robust – not at all runny.

Lay out a sheet of filo pastry with the short edge towards you. Brush it with butter, then top with another sheet and brush with butter again. Turn the sheets over together so you can brush the underside of the original sheet with butter. Take one-sixth of the filling mixture and arrange it in a long sausage along the short end, leaving a border of about 2cm. Fold the border over the filling, then, pinching the side edges together to make sure none of the filling falls out, roll up the whole piece of filo until you have one filled sausage. Set aside and repeat with the remaining filo and filling until you have 6 sausages. Press down lightly so the rolls spread out into any small gaps.

Take the cake tin and, starting in the middle, coil the filo rolls round until the base of the tin is covered. Make the topping by whisking together the eggs and the yoghurt and pour this over the filo sausages, spreading it as evenly as possible. Bake in the oven for about 25 minutes. The top should be lightly puffed up and golden. Remove from the oven. The banitsa can be eaten hot from the oven, or when cooled.

The morning after nets, Harrison Burns is in the Bridge Farm shop, a troubled expression on his face.

'I've sorted the pud. But I'm having real trouble with the main.'

'Yes?' Behind the counter, Helen waited. 'Because . . .?'

'Fallon's such a good cook. I want to do summat impressive. But not too complicated. Can't risk it going wrong.'

'How about steak? We've got some lovely Angus sirloin.'

'Steak's a bit basic, isn't it?'

'Depends what you do with it.'

The door is flung open. Tom enters on a gust of chill February air, a plastic tray grasped in his outstretched arms.

'All right, Harrison?'

'Hiya.'

'Could you . . .?'

'Yeah, no sweat.' Harrison closes the door as Tom upends the tray. Beetroots tumble into a woven display container, the green leaves still attached, veined in rich purple.

'Want some?'

'No, you're all right. Isn't beetroot dead messy to cook?'

'Doesn't have to be. You can wrap it in foil.'

'Goes really nicely with mackerel,' Helen offers.

STUFFED MACKEREL AND WARM BEETROOT SALAD
Serves 4

4 garlic cloves, peeled and crushed
3 tbsp finely chopped parsley
2 tbsp finely chopped dill
1 tsp crushed cumin seeds
olive oil
4 mackerel, cleaned and scaled
1 lemon, very thinly sliced
salt and black pepper

Beetroot salad
4 medium to large beetroots
thyme sprigs
olive oil
sherry vinegar
finely chopped dill

To serve
lemon wedges

First cook the beetroots. Preheat the oven to 200°C/Fan 180°C/Gas 6. Wash the beetroots and wrap each one in a piece of foil with a sprinkling of salt and a sprig of thyme. Put the beetroots on a baking tray and roast for about an hour, or until each one is tender when pierced with a knife. Remove from the oven and set aside.

For the mackerel, turn the oven down to 190°C/Fan 170°C/Gas 5. Mix the crushed garlic with the herbs and cumin seeds and season with salt and pepper. Moisten with a little olive oil to make a paste. Divide this mixture between the mackerel cavities and add a few lemon slices to each one. Lay the mackerel in a baking tray lined with foil, drizzle with olive oil and bake for about 25 minutes or until the fish are cooked through.

Meanwhile, finish the beetroot salad. Unwrap the beetroot, peel off the skins and slice. Dress them with olive oil and sherry vinegar to taste and season with salt and pepper. Sprinkle with a little dill. When the mackerel are ready, serve with the warm beetroot salad and wedges of lemon to squeeze over the fish.

Harrison looks less than convinced. 'Sounds a bit fiddly.'

'OK...'

A sudden thought. 'Hey, Tom, is Roy all right?'

'What do you mean?'

'He was all over the place at nets last night.'

'Oh, you know. Valentine's coming up. Never a good day for him, thinking how things might have been.'

'Yeah. Poor bloke.'

'I'll tell you what he needs to do. Stop listening to Radiohead.'

In the middle of the month, calving starts at Brookfield. When their dairy herd consisted of classic black-and-white Holstein Friesians, this was a very labour-intensive time. But to make the most of their spring calving system, they replaced the Holsteins with a crossbred herd. This is a mix of Jersey, British Friesian and Montbéliarde. You will be familiar with the last one from the purebred Monteys at Bridge Farm. The purpose of this mixture is to combine the best characteristics of each breed. They produce high-quality milk mainly from grass; are long-lived and healthy; and are not too big, so they can be kept out on soggy ground for longer without ruining it. A side effect is that their coats are a wonderful melting pot of all the genetic influences: some all black, some the greyish-brown known as dun, and others an artist's palette of patches.

'This would never have worked with the old herd.'

'Thanks, pet.' Ruth takes the mug of coffee that Pip has brought out to the calving shed. 'Spring calving, you mean?'

'Not once lambing starts as well.'

The other great advantage of these cows is that they calve easily, without much human help. Ruth is looking for the signs that a labour has started. There are physical changes to the back end, and the mum-to-be often behaves strangely. She might separate herself from the others, push her head against a wall, pace and paw at the ground. Well, wouldn't you if you were about to give birth to a calf weighing the thick end of 30 kilograms?

A couple of hours ago, Ruth had put a heifer in a pen on her own, and the animal is now lying on her side.

Despite it being her first pregnancy, she delivers with no trouble. Now officially a cow, she licks the calf all over, and it very quickly struggles to its feet and starts feeding.

'No matter how many times I see it . . .'

'Me too, Mum.'

'There's still something magical about a new life.'

The calves stay with the mothers for a while, to ensure they get a good feed of essential colostrum. Then they are separated out into groups. This separation is an essential part of the dairying process, often much criticised, but the earlier it happens the less the distress for mothers and calves. Ruth and Pip will select some heifer calves as 'replacements', with a future in Brookfield's dairy herd. The other heifers, and the bull calves, will be kept for a couple of weeks before being transported to Borchester's out-of-town cattle market for sale, either for beef or to join other dairy herds. Because the mothers now start to be milked in the parlour, there is an ever-growing number of calves to feed. Twice a day, several calves at once crowd round the teats of the specially designed feeders, which are filled with milk replacement (basically, formula) or whole milk, courtesy of the increasing number of cows now being milked. The replacements will continue in this way, supplemented with some calf nuts and straw, for at least nine weeks.

'I'm home! . . . Harrison!' Fallon drops her keys in the dish on the hall table. Her voice lowers. 'What . . .?'

FEBRUARY

A champagne flute catches the light, streams of tiny bubbles chasing their way up the golden liquid. A piece of card leans against the glass. In Harrison's bold hand, it instructs *DO NOT ENTER THE KITCHEN!* Fallon picks it up. In smaller letters it continues:

Do feel free to quench your thirst. Then book yourself into JK's first.

'Hello, love.'

'Oh, you made me jump!'

Smiling, Harrison approaches and kisses her. 'How did your Valentine teas go?'

'Really good. Packed out.'

'Awesome.'

'What's all this about?' Fallon waves the card in the vague direction of the bubbly.

'I'm cooking, so I've made a little treasure hunt to keep you from interfering.'

'I wasn't going to interfere!'

He smiles. 'To pass the time, then.'

She takes the glass and sips. Her eyes widen. 'This is good stuff.'

'Nothing but the best for you, my love. Give me about twenty minutes.' And with a peck on her cheek, he returns to the kitchen.

Fallon muses as she takes another sip. The fine, biscuity nose confirms that this is no hen party Prosecco. First book herself into JK's. Where on earth is JK's . . .? But if it's 'then', why is it 'first'?

'Very clever!'

Harrison's reply is muffled by the closed kitchen door. 'Can't talk! Cooking!'

Tucked into page 142 of *Harry Potter and the Philosopher's Stone* is another piece of card:

If you're willing to take the next step on your way, seek the visual proof of a plastic-free day.

Easy. Fallon crosses the lounge and takes down from the wall the photo of their wedding day; Harrison so handsome in his suit, she so happy in the vintage dress that Jazzer had helped her choose. Who'd have thought that Jazzer could be such a style guru? She turns the frame round. Sure enough, taped to the back:

Look for the card that is next in the deck, nestling up to my body and neck.

'It is gorgeous.'

'You like it, then?' Harrison can't hide his relief as he carries two full plates to the table. Seated, Fallon extends her wrist. The crystals on her new bracelet glitter in the candlelight.

'That guitar one had me guessing for a while. I thought you meant *your* body and neck.'

'Oh no, I was off limits. Was. Not now.'

Eight clues had led Fallon all round Woodbine Cottage, until the last had drawn her to the jewellery box in their bedroom, and the beautifully wrapped gift.

Harrison carefully places a plate in front of her.

'This looks amazing. You're amazing.'

'You're pretty amazing yourself.' He takes her hand. 'Happy Valentine's Day.'

'Happy Valentine's Day.'

STEAK WITH BORSETSHIRE BLUE CHEESE SAUCE
Serves 2

2 steaks (sirloin or ribeye)

Sauce
25g butter
1 shallot, peeled and very finely chopped
50ml white wine
150ml double cream
50g blue cheese
dash of Worcestershire sauce
salt and black pepper

First make the sauce. Heat the butter in a small pan. When it has melted and started to foam, add the shallot and cook until it is very soft and translucent. Turn up the heat, then add the wine and let it reduce to about a tablespoon.

Turn down the heat and add the cream. When it has heated through, add the blue cheese and stir until it has melted. Season with salt and pepper to taste, then add a dash of Worcestershire sauce. This sauce can be made ahead and reheated gently, adding in any meat juices from the resting steak.

Take the steak out of the fridge at least an hour before you want to cook it – you will get the best results if the steak is at room temperature, not fridge-cold. Pat the steaks dry with kitchen paper and season lightly with salt.

Heat a griddle pan until it is too hot to hold your hand over it, then add the steaks and cook to your preference. For blue, cook for a minute on each side; for rare, 1½ minutes on the first side, then 1 minute on the other; for medium rare, 2 minutes on the first side and 1½ minutes on the second; and for medium, 2 minutes on each side.

Once the steaks are cooked, leave them to rest for at least 5 minutes, then strain any juices into the blue cheese sauce. Serve with some green vegetables or a salad.

RASPBERRY CHEESECAKE
Serves 8

Crust
250g digestive biscuits
125g butter, plus extra for greasing

Filling
350g full-fat cream cheese
225g cottage cheese
140g caster sugar
3 eggs, beaten
1 tsp vanilla extract

Topping
300ml soured cream
1 tbsp caster sugar
2 tbsp fresh lemon juice
punnet of raspberries

Preheat the oven to 170°C/Fan 150°C/Gas 3½.

First make the crust. Crumble the digestive biscuits into a bowl or put them in a plastic bag and bash them with a rolling pin. Melt the butter in a small pan, then add it to the biscuit crumbs and mix well.

Grease a flan dish or a shallow 23cm springform cake tin with butter, then pile in the biscuit mixture and press it down firmly. Put the crust in the fridge to chill while you make the filling.

Put all the filling ingredients in a food processor or blender and blitz until well combined. Carefully pour the filling over the crust, place the tin in the oven and cook for 25–30 minutes. Remove and set aside to cool for an hour.

Preheat the oven to 200°C/Fan 180°C/Gas 6. Mix the soured cream, caster sugar and lemon juice together and spread the topping over the cake. Bake for 5 or 6 minutes, then remove and leave to cool completely.

Before serving, decorate the cake with fresh raspberries – in a heart shape if you like!

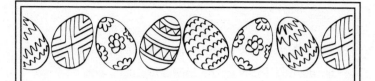

CHAPTER SEVEN

March

The very first day of March – St David's Day – has particular significance for Natasha (née Thomas), who became an Archer by marrying Tom in 2019. Natasha is originally from Cardiff, but her parents now live in north Wales, near Betws-y-Coed.

WELSH FRUIT TEA LOAF
Makes 1 x 900g loaf

375g mixed dried fruit (raisins, currants, sultanas)
100g muscovado sugar
150ml strong black tea
butter, for greasing
225g self-raising flour
2 tsp mixed spice
2 eggs, beaten

Put the dried fruit and sugar in a large bowl. Add the tea and stir well, then leave to soak overnight.

When you're ready to bake the loaf, preheat the oven to 180°C/Fan 160°C/Gas 4. Grease a 900g loaf tin with butter and line it with baking paper.

Sift the flour and mixed spice into the soaked fruit and sugar, then stir in the eggs and mix well until everything is combined.

Spoon the mixture into the prepared loaf tin.

Bake for about 1¼ hours or until the loaf has risen and is golden brown on top. Check that it is done by inserting a skewer into the centre – the skewer should come out clean.

Leave the loaf to cool in the tin for 5 minutes, then turn it out onto a wire rack to finish cooling. Store in an airtight tin and ideally leave for a day or so to mature before eating. It's very nice spread with good Welsh butter.

Natasha got off to a shaky start with her future in-laws. After a career in cosmetics, she set up a successful fruit juice business from her own orchard. When Tom met this high-flyer through the Nuffield Farming Scholarship scheme, his head was turned so strongly that he only narrowly avoided whiplash. He eagerly introduced Natasha to the family, but an early dinner party was not a success. Pat and Tony bridled at her frank opinions on their business. To make things even more awkward, Natasha dislikes cinnamon, so she barely ate any of the main course.

SPICED LAMB
Serves 4

1.5kg shoulder of lamb
1 tsp mustard powder
1 tsp ground ginger
1 tsp ground cinnamon
1 garlic clove, crushed
1 onion, peeled and chopped
2 tbsp Worcestershire sauce
3 tbsp white wine vinegar
3 tbsp tomato purée
1 tbsp sugar
salt and black pepper

Preheat the oven to 190°C/170°C/Gas 5. Trim any excess fat off the lamb and discard it, then place the meat on a large piece of foil in a roasting tin. Mix the mustard, ginger and cinnamon with the crushed garlic to make a paste and spread it over the meat.

Mix the onion with the Worcestershire sauce, vinegar, tomato purée and sugar in a bowl and season with salt and pepper. Pour this mixture over the lamb, then wrap the foil round it to completely enclose it. Put it in the oven and cook for 2½ hours. Serve the lamb with the spicy juices and some baked potatoes and green vegetables.

Despite his parents' wariness, Tom hurtled into the relationship, getting married less than four months later. Natasha
was a prime mover in the Bridge Fresh scheme, going
into business with Tom to develop an app and website to
revolutionise their veg boxes and integrate them with the
products of the Bridge Farm shop. But no matter how
technological the public face, actually producing the stuff
is still a hands-on, soil-under-the-fingernails business. In the
polytunnels today, Johnny and Tom are planting tomatoes
and cucumbers. Tomorrow it will be salad leaves. Brussels
sprouts and cauliflowers are also on the to-do list on Tom's
phone. With a lot of input from Natasha, Tom has expanded
the range to include unusual items like cucamelons and
agretti. But at this time of year they do not have much of
their own produce available. Kale and leeks are still producing, but otherwise it is mainly root vegetables and potatoes
from the store. So to give their customers enough variety,
they buy in a lot of produce from an organic co-operative.

March is a capricious month, which country dwellers
have long respected. Will it be the harbinger of spring, or a
bitter reminder of the cruelty of winter? Or, as is often the
case, a bit of both just to keep us on our toes? Whatever the
weather, in March the efforts of Ambridge's farmers become
more visible to the passer-by. In a field at Home Farm, a
tractor steadily zigzags its lonely pattern. Despite the brisk
easterly, Adam Macy is warm in the cab, with the radio
for company. Through the winter, weeds were allowed to
grow among the stubble of the previous crop, but they were
sprayed off a week ago. Now Adam is drilling spring barley.

Sturdily booted and well wrapped up, Lynda and Robert
Snell have stopped by a blackthorn hedge, still leafless but

shimmering with white blossom. Months later, those flowers will become berries, the essential ingredient of that comforting sloe gin Eddie made in September.

'Apple, Lyndy?'

Robert produces the fruit from his pocket, polishes it on his handkerchief – clean that morning, don't worry – and passes it to his wife. Lynda nibbles daintily. A brave wild daffodil trumpets its delicate yellow in the road verge as they try to dismiss the grumble of the tractor and focus on the birdsong in the nearby copse.

'That's obviously a coal tit, Robert.'

There is no mistaking the high-pitched 'see-you, see-you' up high and out of sight in the needles of an old pine.

'But . . . that one? There?'

'I'm not sure . . . Let's call it a great tit. You know what they say.'

The coal tit's larger cousin can have over ninety different songs. Birders joke that if you are not sure what bird you are hearing, it is probably a great tit.

Unlike the barley being drilled here, much of the arable crops were sown in the autumn. Tomorrow Adam will be top-dressing some of his winter wheat with nitrogen fertiliser. He has invested in a precision spreader that can be used with GPS field mapping to target fertiliser where the crops need it most. It was a big investment, but it will reduce the environmental footprint and cut costs. The plant takes up the nitrogen to form chlorophyll, which it uses to convert light energy into starches and sugars.

Adam has planted a variety of milling wheat, for flour production. If it does not make the grade, it will go for animal feed, which is much less lucrative. So he will treat the emerging plants – straggly grass-like clumps – with tender care. At least, as tender as you can be at the wheel of a 300-horsepower tractor.

Lynda retrieves her own freshly laundered linen handkerchief from a pocket and dabs a jewel of apple juice from the corner of her mouth. She thinks of the apple trees in their garden at Ambridge Hall, and the old saying 'March dust on apple leaf brings all kind of fruit to grief'. No powdery mildew on their trees, thanks to regular watering and careful pruning, she thinks – with just the barest hint of smugness.

'Um . . .'

The apple now reduced to its core, Lynda is having a moment's struggle with her conscience.

'I'm sure it'll be fine if you just chuck it under the hedge,' Robert assures her.

It lands just beyond the glossy heart-shaped leaves of a patch of lesser celandine. This bright yellow flower was much loved by Wordsworth, who wrote three separate poems about it. Rather less poetically, it is also known as pilewort, as it was believed to be a cure for haemorrhoids.

Lynda and Robert stroll off in the direction of Brookfield Farm. A tractor is a regular sight on the fields of Ambridge and one that doesn't raise much joy in their hearts. But little lambs . . . now that is a different proposition altogether. March and tiny sheep go together like (whisper it quietly) roast lamb and mint sauce, although Robert is rather more partial to redcurrant jelly.

In the uncertain world of sheep production, lambing is the most crucial time of the year. Anyone who farms with animals will tell you that where there is livestock there is deadstock. Centuries of practical experience, backed with extensive veterinary research, ensure that the proportion of the second to the first is as low as possible.

When Brian bought Home Farm in 1975, he took over a flock of five hundred ewes. They were mainly Cluns (a breed originating in the Clun Forest in Shropshire) crossed with Suffolks. Farmers producing lamb for the table often work with sheep that have been cross-bred in order to achieve hybrid vigour (a term also familiar to gardeners), and to benefit from the strongest characteristics of each breed. It is very common to cross a lowland ram with a hill or mountain breed to produce a 'mule'. This should not be confused with the offspring of a male donkey and a female horse. The meat of that sort of mule makes a strikingly poor Sunday roast, and you would be a very long time trying to knit a scarf from its wool. The sheep mule is often further crossed with another breed, to achieve the best balance of hardiness, fertility and mothering behaviour.

Brian soon recruited a shepherd: Sammy Whipple. For over twenty years, Sammy and his dogs were to be seen working the flock of sheep with their enigmatic black faces and upright stance. Sammy's modern equivalent is Eli. He takes the lion's share of lambing duties, with Adam fitting in around his other work. Although ewes can give birth during the day, the most common times are around dawn or dusk, or at night. So the lambing shed is staffed from 5 a.m. until midnight or later, and checks are often made overnight as well. Brian is known to lend a hand, although now he is well into his seventies he is not keen on the late shifts. Since the farmhouse was sold, Adam kips in his space-age eco-office to reduce night-time toing and froing.

◇◇◇

Ambridge International

IRELAND

◇◇◇

As 17 March is St Patrick's Day, this is an appropriate time to mention a double Irish connection. When she fell scandalously pregnant in 1967, Jennifer refused to identify the father. But newborn Adam's shock of red hair made it pretty obvious that it was Brookfield Farm's cowman, a roguish Ulsterman by the name of Paddy Redmond.

Many years later, Brian too had an outrageous Irish liaison. Siobhan Hathaway was twenty-two years younger than him and worked as a translator. Brian finally fathered the son he had longed for. But with savage irony, it was not with his wife but with his mistress. He nearly abandoned everything for Siobhan and baby Ruairi. But somehow the pull of Ambridge, the farm and Jennifer proved too much. With superhuman grace, Jennifer managed to forgive him. Siobhan made things a little easier by moving with Ruairi to Germany. But in 2007 she returned, tragically suffering from terminal cancer. It took an immense effort for Jennifer to agree to take the boy in, but she grew to love him as her own. Settling in Ambridge and being sent to an English boarding school removed all trace of Ruairi's Irish accent. But he often thinks of his mother, and his family across the water.

POTATO FARLS
Serves 4

450g floury potatoes
15g butter
125g plain flour, plus extra for dusting
salt and white pepper

Peel the potatoes, cut them into quarters and boil them in salted water until soft. Drain well, then leave them to air-dry for a minute or so. Add the butter and mash until they are as smooth as you can make them, then season well with salt and pepper.

Add the flour and gradually work it in to the mash to make a soft dough. Turn the dough out onto a floured surface and roll it out into a rectangle. Cut the rectangle into triangles.

Heat a non-stick frying pan over a medium heat, then fry the farls for about 3 minutes on each side or until heated through and golden brown in patches. Serve the farls at once on their own with butter, or topped with poached eggs.

Unlike Home Farm, Brookfield has no dedicated shepherd, so lambing there is more of an all-hands-to-the-pump affair – especially as it overlaps with calving, which is still continuing. Ruth, Pip, David and Josh all muck in; Josh rather more reluctantly, as he has his farm machinery business to attend to. Even Ben takes a turn when he can fit it around his college work. Right now Pip is on duty, hoping that Toby is looking after Rosie properly.

In 2016, Toby Fairbrother was enthused by mates at the rugby club who were following the 'caveman diet' – lots of grass-fed meat, but no dairy, cereals or processed foods. Toby persuaded his more cautious brother Rex to go into business marketing pastured eggs, produced by chickens roaming a new section of fresh grass every day. Bert Fry agreed to build them a large wheeled henhouse – the eggmobile – and somehow Justin Elliott entered into a sponsorship deal for the packaging. Always with an eye for the main chance, Josh came on board, leveraging his experience with Neil Carter's more conventional egg business into a sweet fifty-fifty arrangement.

For a while, it looked as if Upper Class Eggs might be a success, supplying the Bridge Farm shop and Ambridge Tearoom among other outlets. But ever reckless and feckless, Toby over-promised a new restaurant client and got into a lot of trouble with a promotional video, learning the hard way that buying a drone doesn't make you the new Spielberg. Detained overnight by one of his amorous adventures, he forgot to shut up the eggmobile and a fox caused carnage among the hens. Eventually, Rex and Josh pulled the plug, although by then Toby was already tinkering with artisan spirits.

Rex and Josh continued with a more conventional free-range egg business, whose products sell at rather less than the eye-watering £3.50 a half-dozen charged for the Upper Class variety. Even with Toby at the helm, that was always going to be a tough sell.

The Feathers is often used by Borsetshire NFU for its lunches and dinners.

DEVILLED EGGS
Makes 12

12 eggs

Filling
4 heaped tbsp mayonnaise
1–2 tsp English or Dijon
  mustard
¼ tsp honey
½ tsp white wine vinegar
a few dashes of
  Worcestershire sauce

a few dashes of Tabasco
salt and white pepper

To garnish
a sprinkle of sweet or hot
  paprika or cayenne
chopped chives or finely
  chopped parsley leaves

First boil the eggs. Put the eggs in a pan and cover them with water. Bring the water to the boil, then immediately turn down the heat to the lowest simmer. Cook for 7 minutes, then drain at once and cool in iced water.

Peel the eggs carefully, then cut them in half and remove the yolks. Put the yolks in a bowl and crumble them until fine. Stir in the mayonnaise, a teaspoon of the mustard, the honey, vinegar, Worcestershire sauce and a dash of tabasco. Season with salt and white pepper. Mix thoroughly – this is easiest done with a stick blender, but you can combine everything very well with a spatula – then taste. Add more mustard and Tabasco if you want the mixture hotter.

You can just spoon the mixture into the cavities of the halved eggs, but it looks much nicer if you pipe it using a star nozzle. Put the mixture into a piping bag and fill the egg cavities with swirls of the mixture, making sure it domes slightly.

Sprinkle each egg with paprika or cayenne and either a few chopped chives or finely chopped parsley.

The Brookfield lambing shed rings with the bleating of mothers and offspring. Pip surveys the ewes that have not yet lambed, looking for the telltale signs. A ewe nearby has stopped eating, seems restless and has separated herself from the others. Another gave birth to one lamb about an hour ago. Most of the ewes manage without much human help, but Pip knows that another lamb should have made an appearance by now. It's time to investigate, so she dons a disposable glove and squelches on some lubricant. Her experienced hand soon diagnoses the problem. The second lamb is stuck, with one leg back. Working with the mum's contractions, Pip eases the lamb back in the uterus and arranges the moving parts into their proper presentation: front legs under the nose, like a diver. With the next contraction, the lamb slops out onto the straw.

Behind the Scenes

In *The Archers* studio, the sound of a lamb being born is achieved with a damp towel (the lamb), a pile of old recording tape (the straw) and a good handful of natural yoghurt (you can work that out for yourself).

The priority is to make sure the lamb is breathing. Pip tickles its nostrils with straw, prompting a sneeze. And here is the mother, licking the gunge off the newcomer and stimulating his muscles and circulation with her tongue. Within minutes the ram lamb wobbles onto his feet and joins his sister in an enthusiastic feed.

That was a fairly straightforward complication – if there can be such a thing. But sometimes even with a successful birth there can be problems, especially with triplets. A ewe only has two teats, so the weakest lamb can miss out on feeding. If Pip cannot persuade another ewe to become a foster parent, then frequent bottle-feeding is the only option. Leonard Berry – 'Jill's fancy man' (™Freddie Pargetter) – was once rendered nearly speechless by an old shepherds' trick. Ruth rushed into the kitchen, flung open the Aga's warming oven and put a newborn in there. It was the equivalent of a neo-natal incubator for the live but weak lamb. Just remember not to close the door.

Sheep farmers try to handle even difficult births themselves, usually only getting into the expense of a vet's visit if the life of the ewe is threatened. Alistair Lloyd is still a regular visitor – he did the ultrasound scans which identified how many lambs each ewe was carrying – but since his split with Shula his visits to Brookfield are now purely professional.

Shula's dissatisfaction with the marriage had been brewing for many years, worsened by Alistair's gambling addiction. But the last straw came in 2018, when she received a small legacy from her friend Caroline Sterling. Desperate to shake things up, she suggested to Alistair that they take an extended working holiday, only to be squashed by his negative reaction. He tried to make amends, but his idea of putting a bit of spice in their life was for them to cook a special meal together. The next morning, she told him it was over.

GOAN FISH CURRY
Serves 4

Fish
juice of 1 lime
1 tsp salt
600g firm white fish fillets, skinned and diced

Spice paste
1 tsp coriander seeds
1 tsp cumin seeds
2cm piece of cinnamon stick

1 star anise

6 dried red Kashmiri chillies (or a tablespoon of Kashmiri
  chilli powder)

3 cloves

4 garlic cloves, crushed

15g fresh root ginger, grated

2 tbsp tamarind purée

Curry

2 tbsp vegetable oil or coconut oil

1 large onion, peeled and finely sliced

1 large tomato, peeled, deseeded and finely chopped

400ml can of coconut milk

chopped coriander, to garnish

salt and black pepper

Temper

1 tbsp vegetable oil

1 tsp mustard seeds

12 curry leaves

Put the lime juice in a bowl with the salt and add the fish. Toss
the fish in the lime juice, then add just enough water to cover.
Leave to stand until you are ready to cook it.

Next make the spice paste. Put all the spices, including the
dried chillies, in a dry frying pan and toast until they smell very
aromatic. Remove from the heat and leave to cool, then grind
to a fine powder. Mix with the garlic, ginger, tamarind purée
and just enough water to make a thick paste.

Heat the oil in a large flameproof casserole dish and add the onion. Cook over a medium heat until slightly softened and turning a light golden brown, then stir in the spice paste. Keep cooking, stirring constantly, for several minutes until it smells intensely aromatic and the paste starts to separate from the oil. Stir in the tomato and stir for a further couple of minutes. Season with salt and pepper.

Pour in the coconut milk along with 200ml of water, then bring to the boil. Simmer for 10–15 minutes until the sauce has reduced a little and turned a richer colour, then drain the fish and add this to the casserole dish. Leave to simmer for 4–5 minutes until the fish is just cooked through.

While the fish is cooking, heat the oil in a frying pan and add the mustard seeds and curry leaves. The curry leaves will crackle and dry very quickly, and the mustard seeds will pop. Stir these into the curry. Garnish with coriander and serve with basmati rice.

Pip leaves the little family to bond, and later will lead them off to their own separate pen, spray-numbered so she knows whose lamb is whose. But they do not stay indoors for long, especially if the weather is good. David is taking yesterday's lambs with their mothers out to a sheltered field near the yard, where they should thrive on fresh grass and occasional sunny spells. But he is alarmed to see Lynda and Robert.

'You haven't got the dog, have you?'

'Fear not, David.' Even when she is being kind, Lynda's

Sunningdale drawl and idiosyncratic phraseology can make people feel patronised. 'We're well aware that it's the lambing season. Monty is at home.'

'Good. Well . . . that's thoughtful of you.'

David leaves the Snells smiling fondly at the ewes and lambs. Most stick close together, but the occasional reckless one makes a bold exploratory foray – until its mother's insistent call urges it to skitter back to safety. As soon as the ground is dry enough underfoot, David will also take the Hereford cattle out, so they can start eating grass instead of expensive winter fodder.

'Robert . . .'

'Yes?'

'You know Easter's coming up soon.'

'Ye–es . . .' Robert has a strong suspicion of what is coming.

'Might you come to the early service, do you think?'

On Easter Sunday, it is traditional for a few of the hardy faithful to join the vicar at dawn on the summit of Lakey Hill. Robert loves his wife with an intensity utterly baffling to most observers. But getting up at 5 a.m. to stand on a chilly hillside? A chap has his limits.

'It's very tempting, but no. No thank you.'

Lynda knows her husband of old. He will indulge her passions and whims with enormous tolerance. But inside that affable exterior – very deep inside – lies a core of steel.

'As you like. Shall we wander home for some tea?'

'Excellent idea, Lyndy. And I've made some buns.'

'Lovely.'

EXTRA FRUITY HOT CROSS BUNS
Makes 12

500g strong white bread flour, plus extra for dusting
75g caster sugar
10g instant yeast
2 tsp salt
40g unsalted butter, softened
2 medium eggs, beaten
120ml whole milk, warm
120ml tepid water
150g sultanas
30g dried cranberries
50g chopped mixed peel
finely grated zest of 2 oranges
1 dessert apple, cored and diced
2 tsp ground cinnamon

Crosses
75g plain flour

Glaze
75g apricot jam

In a large mixing bowl, mix the flour, sugar and yeast. Add the salt, butter, eggs, milk and half the water and mix with your fingers. Work the mixture together, incorporating the flour from the sides of the bowl and adding small amounts of water until you have a rough dough.

Transfer the dough to a lightly floured surface and knead for about 10 minutes or until soft and springy. Dust your bowl with flour and put the dough back in it. Cover with a damp tea towel and leave the dough to prove in a warm place for at least an hour or until it's doubled in size.

Transfer the dough to a lightly floured surface and sprinkle the sultanas, dried cranberries, mixed peel, orange zest, apple and cinnamon on top. Knead for about 10 minutes or until evenly incorporated. Keep folding the dough inwards until all the air is knocked out.

Line a baking tray with baking paper. Divide the dough into 12 pieces and roll each piece into a ball. Place them on the baking tray, spacing them out evenly.

Cover with the damp tea towel and leave in a warm place for up to an hour, or until the dough has at least doubled in size and springs back when touched. Preheat the oven to 220°C/ Fan 200°C/Gas 7.

For the crosses, mix the flour with 75ml of water to make a paste. Using a piping bag fitted with a fine nozzle, pipe crosses onto the buns. Bake in the hot oven for 15–20 minutes, or until golden brown. In a small pan, warm the apricot jam with a splash of water, then sieve and brush over the tops of the warm buns to glaze. Cool on a wire rack.

CHAPTER EIGHT
April

March can retain vestiges of winter, but in April spring definitely takes hold. Longer, stronger sunshine combined with rain (hopefully just the right amount) energises the countryside, which explodes into life. On the farms, there is a definite change of gear. The cattle are outside, the fields are full of growing lambs, and the arable crops need regular checking. Just as gardeners have to be alert to the weeds revitalised by the advancing season, there are lots of pests and diseases queueing up to make life difficult for Adam, so he will consult with the agronomist regularly. At Brookfield and Home Farm, lambing will finish by the middle of the month. Eli can catch up on his sleep, and maybe even dream of his favourite dish.

SHEPHERD'S PIE

Serves 4

2 tbsp olive oil
1 onion, peeled and chopped
1 celery stick, chopped
2 carrots, peeled and chopped
2 garlic cloves, peeled and chopped
600g leftover roast lamb, diced, or lamb mince
100ml red wine
300ml lamb or chicken stock
1 tbsp tomato purée
thyme sprig

1 bay leaf
Worcestershire sauce
salt and black pepper

Mashed potato topping
1kg floury potatoes (such as Maris Pipers), peeled and
  quartered
30g butter, plus extra for dotting over the top
a little warm milk (optional)

Heat the oil in a large frying pan, add the onion, celery and
carrots and cook for 5–10 minutes until softened. Add the
garlic and cook for another few minutes, then add the meat
and fry until nicely browned. Now pour in the red wine and
let it bubble for a few moments, then add the stock, tomato
purée, herbs and a splash of Worcestershire sauce. Season with
salt and pepper, then cover the pan and leave everything to
cook for about 15 minutes.

Boil the potatoes in salted water until tender, then drain and tip
them back into the pan and let them dry for a minute or so. Mash
with the butter and a little warm milk if needed, then season with
salt and pepper. Preheat the oven to 200°C/Fan 180°C/Gas 6.

Pile the filling mixture into a baking dish or pie dish and
cover with the mash. Dot with butter, then bake for about 30
minutes or until the filling is bubbling and the top is beautifully
browned. Serve with some green vegetables.

APRIL

With the grass thriving and calving coming to an end, milk production is intensifying. As the tides dominate a beach, the morning-and-evening task of milking shapes the day on a dairy farm. There is even a twice-daily tidal flow, as the cows are brought to and from the milking parlour. Ruth and Pip are the milking maestras, but the three Brookfield menfolk are all competent and can step in when needed. (I am not including Toby here, who is barely competent to put his own trousers on.)

With a mug of strong tea inside her, and blinking the sleep from her eyes, Ruth drives the cows to the collecting yard. They know the drill. The same pushy few will usually lead the herd.

'No you don't . . .'

With a slap on the rump, Ruth urges on the daydreamer easily distracted by a spray of primroses in the hedgebank, and the awkward so-and-so eyeing up the escape routes.

The first twenty cows enter the parlour and settle in on two sides, facing outwards. An automatic system identifies each cow and dispenses an appropriate ration for her to munch on. It also sounds an alarm if she has been treated with medication, so her milk will not flow into the bulk tank with the rest. In the olden days, some sticky tape round her tail sufficed. And tape is still used to warn if madam is prone to kick out – particularly useful if you employ contract or relief milkers, who may not know the herd well.

No such uncertainty for Ruth, who works her way along the familiar udders. She cleans them and attaches

the milking machine's shiny long alloy tubes – the cups –
to each teat. When the machine detects that the cow has
given her milk, the cluster of cups detaches automatically,
and the computer records her milk yield. And then the
clever mechanical bit: the rapid exit system. This was a big
innovation of the new parlour, championed by Pip and
installed in 2019. At the touch of a button, a hydraulic barrier in front of the cows lifts up, and they saunter forward
into another yard. No queueing, no waiting, and the next
batch enters behind them. It might seem simple, but it has
knocked two hours off the working day.

At Bridge Farm, Johnny is performing a similar task,
although on a much smaller scale (fewer cows that is, not
miniature ones). But after each cow has been milked, he
rubs peppermint udder cream into her teats, to prevent
cracking and stimulate circulation. This is quite common
on organic dairy farms, so if you ever meet a farmer
whose hands smell of toothpaste, you can astound them
by identifying their specialism.

Pete the gamekeeper is up early too, doing his rounds
in Leader's Wood. The nearby Millennium Wood was
planted in 2000. But Leader's is ancient woodland, as you
can tell from the carpet of wild garlic, with its vibrant
green leaves and white flower clusters. Actually, you could
tell with your eyes closed, because it smells like an Italian
restaurant in there. But Pete is not a particularly sensual
being. His mind is on a more prosaic task, retrieving
pheasant eggs from the laying pens and taking them to the
incubator. The trees around him are back in bud, greening

up. He remembers an old country saying: 'oak before ash, we'll have a splash; ash before oak, in for a soak'. To be honest, it is not much use as a weather forecast. But it does indicate how early the season is warming, as oaks are more sensitive to temperature than ash.

Horticulturalists agree with T. S. Eliot when he wrote 'April is the cruellest month', because from now until early June we are in the Hungry Gap. Climate change may alter things, but for centuries Britain's winter temperatures limited how soon crops could be sown. And ironically, the spring temperatures encourage hardy winter crops – kale, cauliflowers, sprouts – to direct their energies to produce flowers and seeds: so-called 'bolting'. For centuries at this time of year, people relied on a dreary round of cabbages, potatoes and what they could preserve and eke out over the winter.

Thanks to the supermarkets' global buying power, air transport of perishable produce like soft fruit, and greenhouses using artificial heat, we have become distanced from the seasons. But British rhubarb is an exception to the paucity of home-grown spring produce. Forced rhubarb, grown in the dark, has been available since January. But now, early outdoor varieties become available, and in April it is the closest thing to a locally grown fruit that we have.

RHUBARB CRUMBLE

Serves 4

500g rhubarb
75g soft brown sugar
a few balls of stem ginger in syrup (optional)

Crumble topping
100g plain flour
50g ground almonds
100g sugar
125g butter, cut into cubes

First make the topping. Mix the flour, ground almonds and sugar in a bowl. Add the cubes of butter and rub them in with your fingertips until the mixture has the consistency of breadcrumbs. Set aside.

Cut the rhubarb into pieces roughly 5cm long, removing any damaged bits. Pile these into a pie dish and add the sugar. Toss the rhubarb so it is all coated in the sugar. Add the stem ginger, if using, and stir that into the rhubarb.

Preheat the oven to 200°C/Fan 180°C/Gas 6. Spread the crumble topping over the rhubarb and bake for 35–40 minutes or until the top is golden brown and crunchy and the rhubarb is tender and bubbling up at the sides. Serve with proper custard (see page 230).

Encouraged out by the sunshine, a comma butterfly skitters and jinks, while far overhead a party of swifts screams past, silhouetted against the blue. Tom is making the most of the improving conditions with his planting, as are the gardeners of Ambridge. On veg patches and allotments all over the village, beetroot, lettuce, carrots, spinach, radishes and peas are going in. Tom is also jazzing up the potatoes that will be on offer through Bridge Fresh. He supplements the standard varieties like Sante and Golden Wonder with colourful upstarts, including the variegated Pink Gypsy and Highland Burgundy – as red to the core as a *Socialist Worker* seller.

'Thanks! See you!' The milk tanker lorry, which Ruth is waving off from Brookfield, is taking the contents of their bulk tank to the processor. Bridge Farm's milk has a much shorter journey: just across the yard to the dairy and cheese room.

Nutrition is crucial for dairy cattle. What they eat directly affects the quality of their milk, and therefore the taste and quality of the products made by Helen and her dairy workers, Clarrie Grundy and Susan Carter. In particular, the semi-mystical process of cheesemaking, as much art as science, is very reliant on the raw material. Helen discovered this to her cost in 2018 when, despite their friendship, Ian Craig removed her Borsetshire Blue cheese from Grey Gables' cheeseboard. Helen concluded that the quality of the milk they had been buying in, although organic, was simply too bland to generate the complex and distinctive taste previously associated with her once award-winning cheese. Her solution was radical: to return to in-house milk production, with a new dairy herd of Montbéliarde cows. This French breed is particularly associated with cheese. It is the only milk allowed to be used for the creamy, nutty Comté, a speciality of the mountainous Jura region.

'That's £12.73 please. Contactless?' Helen is serving in the Bridge Farm shop. The life of a cheesemaker is not unlike that of a triangle player in an orchestra, with long periods waiting for the next frantic burst of activity. A timer in her pocket, Helen gets on with other work until summoned by the insistent bleep back to the dairy.

Blue cheese is basically acidified, coagulated, chopped up, squashed, salted, mouldy old milk. And when you put it like that, it is hard to believe how wonderfully tasty it can be. Helen starts the process by warming the milk and then adding a bacterial culture. This changes the sugar (lactose) into lactic acid, contributes to the finished flavour and is the source of the blue veins. Helen now has a couple of hours to wait while the milk solidifies into curds, which she then helps further by adding rennet. Another pause. When her timer pings, Helen drops everything again. She rushes back, each time donning her dairy whites, including hairnet and hat, and cuts the curds with a wire rake. This releases more of the liquid, which after another wait she drains off. The liquid is whey, which Toby once identified as a raw material for an unlikely sounding 'milk gin'. Next, Helen scoops the cut curds into round moulds, and adds salt, which helps preserve the cheese and adds to the flavour.

Helen then pierces the full-size wheels of cheese, plunging many tiny needles into them. This creates air channels in which the mould will grow and flourish, forming the characteristic veins. Finally the cheeses are allowed to mature, turned by hand every week so they dry evenly, with the salt properly distributed and the rind perfectly formed. The whole process is essentially a multi-part biochemical experiment, with the possibility of a taste-affecting variation at any stage. It is no wonder that Helen can seem uptight at times.

Fortunately, Ian loved the new Borsetshire Blue, so it has returned to Grey Gables. You can find it on their cheeseboard, and sometimes in their cooking as well.

BROCCOLI AND BORSETSHIRE BLUE CHEESE SOUP

Serves 4

1 head of broccoli
(about 750g)
1 tbsp butter
1 tbsp olive oil
1 large onion, peeled
and chopped
1 celery stick
1 large floury potato,
peeled and chopped

1 litre vegetable stock
freshly grated nutmeg
150g Borsetshire Blue
cheese, or another
blue cheese, such as
Stichelton, crumbled
salt and black pepper

Chop the broccoli stalk into small pieces and separate out the florets. Set aside.

Heat the butter and oil in a large pan, add the onion and cook until soft and translucent. Don't allow it to brown. Add the chopped broccoli stalks, celery and potato, cook for a few minutes, then pour in the stock. Bring to a simmer and continue to cook for about 15 minutes until the potato is soft. Add the broccoli florets and cook for another 5–10 minutes until tender.

Blitz the soup in a blender or with a hand-held blender until smooth but still flecked with green. Season with a little nutmeg and salt and pepper, then stir in the crumbled blue cheese. Allow it to melt into the hot soup, then serve with some crusty bread.

At Rickyard Cottage, across the yard from Brookfield's farmhouse, Pip is killing some time before afternoon milking. As Rosie plays nearby, she flicks through an old diary. Mortified at the picture it portrays of her gauche younger self, she vows never to let her brothers get their hands on it. Pip turns to tomorrow's date, 23 April. Obscuring the grey print of 'St George's Day (England)' are two words in her loopy primary school handwriting: 'Grandad's birthday'.

'Pip, what is it?' Jill was briskly washing a baking tray, until brought up short by Pip's expression.

'I miss Grandad.'

'Oh, darling . . .' Hands still bejewelled with soap suds, Jill enfolds her in a hug. 'So do I.'

'It's so sad that he never met Rosie.'

'It is. He'd have loved her so much.'

Jill knows that a pot of tea does not cure sadness, but it can ease it a little. Sitting at the kitchen table, the two women agree to take Rosie tomorrow to help put flowers on Phil's grave.

'Does Leonard mind?'

'No, of course not. He does the same for his wife. It doesn't affect how we feel about each other.' Jill nudges a plate. 'Go on, have one of these.'

If there's one thing more comforting than a pot of tea, it is a pot of tea and some home baking.

CHOCOLATE AND WALNUT BROWNIES
Makes 15 squares

200g butter, cut into cubes, plus extra for greasing
25g dark chocolate (70 per cent cocoa solids), broken into
  pieces
3 large eggs
200g golden caster sugar
100g plain flour
100g walnuts, roughly chopped

Grease a 20 x 20cm baking tin with butter and line it with baking parchment. Preheat the oven to 160°C/Fan 140°C/Gas 3.

Put the butter and chocolate in a bowl and set it over a pan of simmering water – the bottom of the bowl should not touch the water. Remove when the butter and chocolate have both melted and set aside to cool slightly.

Break the eggs into a separate bowl, add the sugar, then beat with an electric whisk until the mixture is really pale and creamy. Add the melted chocolate and butter and stir until everything is incorporated, then gently fold in the flour and walnuts.

Pour the mixture into the prepared tin and bake for 25 minutes. The cake will still look quite soft and squishy but will firm up as it cools, so don't be tempted to leave it for longer. Leave to cool in the tin, then cut it into squares to serve.

Behind the Scenes

23 April was also the real-life birthday of Norman Painting, who played Phil Archer from the very first episode in January 1951 to his final appearance in November 2009. For this remarkable achievement, he was celebrated in *The Guinness Book of Records* as the longest-serving actor in a single role.

'Fish poo salad' was how Kate described the produce from Adam's aquaponics system, but don't let that put you off. She was drunk. And you don't want to take much notice of Kate, even when she's sober. Adam grew strawberries at Home Farm for fifteen years. But the increasing difficulty of recruiting and managing pickers finally forced him into abandoning the job. He retained the cherry trees, as cherries have a much shorter season, and the picking can be done by contract labour. But this left him with a large area of polytunnels feeling unwanted.

Aquaponics was Adam's solution. It appealed to him because it is a way of producing both a vegetable crop and a protein one without depleting precious soil. It is an almost closed system, combining fish raised in, well . . .

fish tanks, and leafy salad vegetables grown hydroponi-
cally, their roots in water. The fish Adam has chosen are
tilapia, which grow to half a kilo in five or six months.
Jazzer feeds them on plant-based food, plus worms raised
in a wormery in the polytunnel. The waste matter from
the fish (yes, all right, Kate, the poo) then goes through a
biofilter containing bacteria, which convert it to nutrients
for the plants. The plants further purify the water, which
goes back into the fish tanks.

Tilapia are the most popular choice for this sort of system because they are hardy, thrive on a mainly plant-based
diet and are fine in crowded conditions. They do need
warm water, though (about 30°C), so Adam has set up an
air source heat pump. It is a simple concept in principle,
but does need constant testing and monitoring. Jazzer is
kept busy, making sure all the kit is working properly and
that the plants and fish are doing well.

A Birmingham wholesaler takes most of the full-sized
fish. Adam sells the rest, along with the high-value niche
salad vegetables, to local shops and restaurants – including Grey Gables. Tilapia have a mild-flavoured soft white
flesh. They can be simply pan-fried and served with butter
and lemon, or combined with other fish in a luxurious pie.
And if you serve it with salad greens, Adam will be doubly
pleased.

LUXURY FISHERMAN'S BAKE
Serves 4–6

Topping
1.5kg floury potatoes, peeled and quartered
50g butter, cubed, plus extra for dotting on top
100g Cheddar cheese, grated

Filling
4 eggs
500ml milk
2 bay leaves
500g monkfish or tilapia, skinned and boned
200g smoked haddock fillet, skinned
50g butter
50g plain flour
freshly grated nutmeg
200g frozen peas, defrosted
2 tbsp finely chopped parsley
salt and black pepper

Put the potatoes in a large pan of water, add salt and bring
to the boil. Cook for 15–20 minutes or until the potatoes are
tender. Drain, then tip them back into the pan and mash well
with the butter. Season with salt and pepper and stir in the
grated cheese. Set aside.

Put the eggs in a pan of cold water and bring to the boil. Turn the heat down to a gentle simmer and cook for 8 minutes. Drain, then put the eggs in a bowl of iced water and set aside.

Pour the milk into a wide pan and bring it to a simmer. Add the bay leaves and the fish, then season with salt and pepper. Cover the pan and simmer the fish for 2 or 3 minutes, then take the pan off the heat and leave to stand for 5 minutes. Remove the fish with a slotted spoon and set it aside. Remove the bay leaves and reserve the cooking liquid.

Preheat the oven to 200°C/Fan 180°C/Gas 6. Melt the butter in a pan, stir in the flour and cook for a minute or so. Add the cooking liquid from the fish and cook for about 5 minutes, stirring constantly, until the sauce has thickened. Season with nutmeg, salt and pepper, then stir in the peas. Peel the eggs and cut them in half.

Spread half the sauce over the base of an ovenproof dish. Add the fish, flaking it into large pieces as you go, then add the eggs. Cover with the rest of the sauce and sprinkle with the chopped parsley.

Spread the mash over the pie, rough it up with a fork and dot with butter. Bake the pie for 25–30 minutes or until the filling is hot and bubbling and the potato topping is brown and crispy.

___

◇◇

Ambridge International

SOUTH AFRICA

◇◇

Kate's children live 8,000 miles away in Durban so her main contact with them is via Skype or FaceTime. They both have Xhosa names, the tribal language of her ex-husband Lucas Madikane. Sipho means 'gift' and Noluthando (call her Nolly now at your peril) means 'one who is loved'. The way Kate often behaves can belie those meanings, although she would protest that she loves them absolutely – in her own way. At least they can rely on the care of Lucas's new wife Siphiwe ('we were given') and his parents, Michael, which means 'who is like God?', and Delia, meaning 'celebrity chef who makes everything simple and supports Norwich City'.

SOUTH AFRICAN BANANA BREAD
Makes 1 loaf

120g butter, at room temperature, plus extra for greasing
175g sugar
1 tsp vanilla extract (optional)
2 eggs
250g plain flour
2 tsp baking powder
pinch of salt
5 ripe bananas, peeled and mashed
100g walnuts, roughly chopped

Preheat the oven to 180°C/Fan 160°C/Gas 4. Grease a small loaf tin with butter.

Beat the butter and sugar in a bowl until really soft and creamy, then add the vanilla extract, if using. Beat in the eggs one at a time, adding a spoonful of the flour in between each one. Fold in the rest of the flour, the baking powder and the salt, then add the mashed bananas and the walnuts and mix well.

Spoon the mixture into the prepared tin and bake for about 50 minutes or until a skewer inserted into the centre comes out clean. Leave the loaf to cool in the tin for 10 minutes, then turn it out onto a wire rack to cool completely.

Serve sliced as it is or spread with butter.

APRIL

'There you go.'

The last cows leave the milking parlour and join the rest of the herd in the yard, shadows long in the evening sunshine. Pip starts the wash down, looking forward to her visit to the churchyard tomorrow. She wonders what the future will bring for little Rosie. Might she one day be standing here, passing on her expertise to her daughter, the future of Brookfield Farm?

Only time will tell . . .

CHAPTER NINE

May

The wheeze of a melodeon is answered with percussive punctuation, as the sticks wielded by Edgeley Morris clatter in the sunshine. It is the first of May – May Day – and the people of Ambridge are marking it in traditional style, perusing the attractions on the village green in floral frocks and ill-advised shorts. The dancers rattle on. Any bashed knuckles will be anaesthetised later, courtesy of The Bull's beer tent, and energies restored with a generous wedge from that essential of every Ambridge fete: the cake stall.

DARK CHOCOLATE CAKE
Makes 10–12 slices

140g unsalted butter, at room temperature, plus extra for
  greasing
200g plain flour
240g caster sugar
1¾ tsp bicarbonate of soda
¼ tsp salt
¼ tsp cream of tartar
50g cocoa powder
240ml milk
1 tsp vanilla extract
2 eggs

Icing
120g butter
**120g dark chocolate (70 per cent cocoa solids), broken up
  into pieces**
about 250g icing sugar
chocolate sprinkles or grated chocolate, to decorate

Grease 2 x 20cm sandwich tins with butter and line them with baking paper. Preheat the oven to 180°C/Fan 160°C/Gas 4.

Sift the flour, sugar, bicarbonate of soda, salt, cream of tartar and cocoa powder into a large bowl and stir. Add the softened butter, milk and vanilla and beat for at least one minute with an electric beater or for 5–10 minutes by hand. Add the eggs, one at a time, beating after each addition.

Divide the mixture between the prepared tins and bake for 25–30 minutes until risen and springy to the touch. Cool in the tins for a few minutes, then turn the cakes out on to a wire rack to cool completely.

For the icing, put the butter and chocolate in a bowl and set it over a pan of simmering water – the bottom of the bowl should not touch the water. Remove when the butter and chocolate have both melted and set aside to cool slightly. Sift the icing sugar and stir it into the chocolate mixture until you have the consistency you desire.

Spread half the icing on top of one cake and sandwich it with the other. Spread the remaining icing over the top. Decorate with chocolate sprinkles or grated chocolate.

MAY

Floralia, Beltane, Rogationtide . . . this optimistic time of
year has been marked for millennia with festivals (Roman,
Celtic and Christian respectively). With spring strutting
like a dandy, and summer polishing its shoes ready for
a grand entrance, the theme of them all is fertility – of
plants, animals and humans.

As well as the Morris, Ambridge's May Day celebrations invariably feature maypole dancing, usually organised
by Lynda Snell. In 2006, she recruited ten-year-old Jamie
Perks as one of the dancers. On the way to a rehearsal,
Jamie asked Kenton (then his mother's partner) about the
true meaning of the maypole. Kenton was lost for words
– unusually but also understandably, because the phallic
symbolism of the pole is so strong that even a stand-up
comic entertaining a stag night might think it a bit unsubtle.

'Hey, dozy! Time to get up!'

All Lily can see of her brother is an exclamation mark
of hair on the pillow. She grabs the duvet and whisks it off
in a single motion.

'What are you *doing*?' In crumpled T-shirt and boxers,
Freddie peers through sleep-encrusted eyes.

'It's four o'clock. If we're going to get to this dawn
chorus thing . . .'

Freddie groans and rolls over. Today is the first Sunday
in May: International Dawn Chorus Day. It is many years
since Lower Loxley hosted dawn chorus walks, and in

recent times they have taken place in woods three miles away in Ambridge. Desperate to exploit any possible source of revenue, Elizabeth has persuaded Kirsty Miller to relocate them to Lower Loxley's arboretum. But bookings for the first event have been on the slim side, so Elizabeth has coerced the family into making up the numbers.

'Freddie, don't go back to sleep!'

'Go on without me. I'd only hold you back.'

'This isn't a war film, and you're not a wounded soldier . . . Come on, we promised Mum.'

Fertility is most definitely on the minds of our dairy farmers, as now is the time to get the cows back in calf. In Tarbutts, a field at the heart of Bridge Farm, you may see one of the Montbéliardes mounting another. But this is not, as you might think, an act of mating, as they are both females. The oestrogen surging through a cow in heat prompts her to mimic the action of a bull, which is why this is known as 'bulling'. If the recipient is not ready, then she will struggle away. But if she stands and tolerates the behaviour, it shows that she is on heat herself. As Johnny cannot always be around to observe this, he has applied a special paint on the top of their tails. It is rather like sheep raddle, but works the other way around.

Most of the cows (or heifers, if they are first-timers) at Bridge Farm and Brookfield will be fertilised via artificial insemination. Johnny will bring in a specialist technician, but Ruth is qualified to perform the task herself. As well as being a more certain process than simply hoping the on-farm bull will do the job, it means they can select beneficial genetic characteristics from bulls anywhere in the world. The (let's not mince our words here) semen comes in straws rather like a ballpoint pen refill. These are chilled until needed in a flask of liquid nitrogen. But after thawing Ruth keeps each one warm by popping it down the back of her boiler suit. And if you think that is an odd way to earn a living, the actual delivery of the vital material is even more so.

Most of the Bridge Farm Montbéliardes will be AI'd. But Johnny will let the Angus bull run with them, as a 'sweeper', in case there are any in which the AI did not take. After all, the bull knows best when a cow is coming into heat, and the crossbred offspring will be perfect for their beef sales. Alistair will visit both farms regularly with a portable ultrasound machine, to do pregnancy diagnoses – usually referred to as PDs.

Freddie keeps up a sustained grumbling as he and Lily pad over the damp grass. 'It's still dark!'

'Mum said we had to be there by half four. The first birds start an hour before sunrise.'

'I thought it was the dawn chorus, not the middle-of-the-night chorus.'

'Keep your voice down.'

In a clearing, a single torch illuminates a small group
of warmly clad locals. With bleary but hopeful eyes, they
gaze pointlessly around them into the woods, dark as a
poacher's jacket. Elizabeth quietly introduces Kirsty, and
steps aside to joins the twins. 'Thank you for coming,'
she whispers. 'I'll treat you to breakfast in the Orangery
afterwards.'

'Maybe lunch,' replies Freddie. 'I'm going back to bed
as soon as I can.'

Kirsty speaks quietly but with an enthusiastic authority.
'You're probably wondering why the birds sing so early.'

'Too right. Hey!' Freddie recoils from a sisterly dig in
the ribs.

'Partly it's to attract a mate, and partly it's to defend
their territory. Singing takes a lot of energy, so this is a
good time to do it, before it's light enough to feed, but
while—'

An extemporary phrase pierces the misty air. Kirsty's
voice drops even lower. 'But while the air is still. Sound
travels much better. Up to twenty times as far.'

The mellow phrase repeats, ending in a chirrup this
time.

'That's a blackbird.' Heads are cocked as a variation of
the same song rings from deeper in the wood. 'They're often
the first up because they have big eyes, so they don't need as
much light to see insects. Anyway, I'll shut up for a bit.'

The blackbirds are soon joined by robins, and the
'swee swee swee' of wrens, implausibly strident for such
small birds. As the light grows, the trees gradually take

on perceptible forms. But focused on the growing counterpoint, some with their eyes closed, the listeners are unaware of the sharpening picture around them. One by one, song thrush, blackcap and chiffchaff join the exultation, underpinned by the wood-flute coo of pigeons and the call to arms of a distant cockerel. Before long, the rising sun is taking hold. It splays misty searchlights through the trees and turns the forest floor into a nightclub lightshow, as the wood echoes to a psychedelic profusion of song.

Behind the Scenes

The BBC's extensive collection of recorded sound effects is now held digitally, but they were originally on gramophone records. So in radio drama they are still known as 'gram effects' or 'grams'. To ensure that the birdsong heard in *The Archers* is correct for the region (the English Midlands) and each season, we asked experts from the RSPB to listen to the entire British birdsong collection and annotate each one.

Eventually, the music fades in a gradual diminuendo. Kirsty gently breaks the silence. 'This is quite normal. There's an old country saying that the birds are at prayers now. But they'll start again in a bit, and if you hang around you'll hear some different ones, too.'

Elizabeth turns to the twins. 'If you want to go back to bed . . .'

'Um . . . no, that's all right.' Freddie has an altered look about him, shriven of all his earlier grumpiness.

'Are you OK, Freddie?'

'I'm fine. I just thought I might stay for the, you know, the next bit.'

'All right. Well, that's great . . .'

Studiously ignoring his sister's quizzical look, Freddie takes a breath of cool morning air.

'It's quite something, isn't it? I had no idea . . .'

Finally, squinting against the morning sun, the Pargetters return to the house in companionable silence. Freddie goes back to bed and sleeps dreamlessly for most of the morning. But he is up in time to hold his mother to that promised lunch.

SALMON EN CROUTE

Serves 6

2 x 500g salmon fillets,
  skinned
250g frozen spinach
  leaves, defrosted
small bunch of parsley
a few tarragon sprigs
zest of 1 lemon

25g butter
2 tbsp wholegrain
  mustard
500g puff pastry
1 egg, beaten
salt and black pepper

Preheat the oven to 200°C/Fan 180°C/Gas 6.

Run your finger over the salmon fillets to check for any pin bones. If you find any, remove them with tweezers.

Squeeze as much water out of the spinach as you can, then chop it finely. Finely chop the parsley and tarragon leaves. Mix the spinach, herbs, lemon zest and butter together and season with plenty of salt and pepper, then spread the mixture over one of the fillets. Spread the mustard over one side of the other salmon fillet, then sandwich the two together, with the mustard facing the spinach mix.

Roll out the puff pastry to a rectangle large enough to completely enclose your salmon. Place the salmon in the middle of the pastry, then brush the exposed sides of pastry with beaten egg. Bring the sides of the pastry up round the salmon, creating a parcel, then very carefully turn the parcel over so the seam is on the bottom. Transfer this to a baking tray.

Brush the pastry with more beaten egg and score lines across the top. Bake in the oven for 35–40 minutes until the pastry is golden brown and puffed up and the salmon is cooked. To check, insert a skewer into the thickest part of the parcel – it should feel hot to touch.

Serve with salad or green vegetables.

While Freddie is drifting away, Ed Grundy's working day is starting. It's going to be a hot one, he thinks ruefully, because today he and Jazzer are shearing Home Farm's sheep. They manoeuvre their special trailer into position, the ewes and lambs in the nearby shed bleating their own plaintive dawn chorus.

The two men are soon sweating in their strong high-waisted shearing jeans, sheepskin moccasins and singlets. Ed pulls a struggling ewe into position and tips her backwards so her shoulders and neck are resting against his legs. With deft, long strokes – 'blows' – of the electric clippers, he removes the fleece in one piece, avoiding any nicks or second strokes. It is only a couple of minutes before the shorn sheep scampers away. She will be much more comfortable through the summer now, and less likely to host potentially nasty bugs.

'Come on, Brian!'

Adam has roped his stepfather in for a couple of hours, and he's finding it hard to keep pace. Brian grabs the shorn fleece, rolls it up and squashes it down with others in a woolsack. 'Shall we stop for a second?' he asks hopefully. 'Jenny's organised some drinks for us.'

Jazzer's ears almost visibly prick up. But he turns his sheep and makes his last few blows, clearing the last of the wool from the hindquarters before straightening up. What will it be? Squash? Shandy? Lemonade? He could murder an Irn-Bru . . .

ELDERFLOWER WINE
Makes 5 or 6 bottles

8 large elderflower heads
4 litres still mineral water
500g granulated sugar
2 tbsp white wine vinegar
juice of 2 lemons

Bring the water to the boil, add the sugar and stir until it has all dissolved. Remove from the heat and leave to cool.

Rinse the elderflower heads and add them to the water and sugar, then stir in the lemon juice and vinegar. Cover and leave for 24 hours.

Strain the liquid through a sieve lined with muslin, squeezing the flowers as you do so. Decant into sterilised screw top bottles and store for 2 weeks before drinking.

Ambridge International
KENYA

Adam read Agricultural Economics at Newcastle University, graduating in 1990, but it was not until 2003 that he started to work at Home Farm. Until then, he was travelling in Africa working on development projects. He was particularly proud of his success in Kenya, where he improved milk yields by crossing local goats with British breeds.

Kenya's capital Nairobi is also the last resting place of soldier and big game hunter Teddy Antrobus. His widow Marjorie settled in Ambridge, bringing a sizeable pack of Afghan hounds and a repertoire of exotic dishes gleaned from a lifetime as a colonial wife. To help with costs, 'Mrs A' also took in lodgers, including a young agricultural student who was getting work experience at Brookfield Farm. David was hotly opposed to the idea of a female trainee, but his resentment of Ruth Pritchard was not to last. Reader, she married him.

KENYAN CHICKEN CURRY
Serves 4

2 tbsp vegetable oil
2 tsp cumin seeds
2 onions, peeled and finely sliced
4 garlic cloves, crushed
15g fresh root ginger, grated
1½ tbsp mild curry powder OR 1 tsp turmeric, 1 tsp
    ground coriander, ½ tsp cinnamon, ½ tsp ground
    cardamom and ½ tsp ground fenugreek
8 bone-in chicken thighs, skinned
2 tomatoes, skinned and finely chopped
400g can of coconut milk
1 tsp honey
1 tbsp lemon juice
salt and black pepper

To serve
green chillies, chopped, to garnish
chopped coriander
basmati rice and/or chapatis

Heat the oil in a large flameproof casserole dish or a sauté pan. Add the cumin seeds and cook for 30 seconds, then add the onions. Cook over a medium heat until the onions are starting to soften and lightly colour, then add the garlic, ginger and spices.

Stir to combine, then add the chicken thighs. Cook for a few minutes, turning the chicken thighs over at intervals so they are completely covered in the spices, then add the tomatoes and the coconut milk.

Season with salt and pepper, then bring to the boil. Turn down the heat and simmer, partially covered with a lid, until the sauce has thickened and the chicken is completely cooked through. Stir in the honey and lemon juice and cook for a further 2 minutes.

Garnish with green chillies and coriander and serve with basmati rice and/or warm chapatis.

Meanwhile at Brookfield, while Ruth is carefully navigating a cow's private parts in the name of artificial insemination, David has enlisted Pip and Josh to help prepare the silage clamp. In January we saw how important silage is in keeping livestock fed through the winter, and this is the start of the process. David has patched up any cracks in the concrete, and they are now lining its floor and three walls with black polythene. David and Pip have been keeping a close eye on the pastures they have earmarked for cutting. They are hoping for some helpful weather and have to liaise closely with Adam, who does some of the work under contract.

MAY

When the team agrees the time is right, they mow the grass and spread it out to wilt. Next day they gather it into lines, and Adam uses his forage harvester to collect it up and chop it finely. As the harvester works up and down the rows, a tractor runs in lockstep alongside, towing a trailer. A chute arcs out from the harvester like the antenna of a giant insect, and the grass is blown through it into the trailer. Meanwhile, another tractor and trailer is returning, having dumped its precious green load into the clamp. There is no time to waste, so the trailers circulate constantly to keep the harvester working. Silage making brings long, relentless days.

Once the grass is in the clamp, it needs to be squashed to expel as much air as possible, by driving a tractor to and fro over it. When Tony used to do this at Bridge Farm, Pat could never bear to watch the vehicle precariously advancing and reversing, high on the heap. After their son John's death in the unprotected seat of Tony's vintage Ferguson, the fear could only intensify. But Tony knows what he is doing and always completes the job safely.

Finally, the team covers the clamp with more plastic sheeting, and weighs it down with old tyres. This is not the only time Brookfield will make silage this year. They plan to get a second cut, to supplement what is now fermenting nicely in the clamp.

Ambridge farmers also make silage in large round bales, individually plastic-wrapped, which are handier to take out to animals in the fields. Those shiny, black cylinders in enigmatic heaps are strangely alien in appearance. But they give livestock farmers the same sense of security that a full larder gives to villagers like Peggy Woolley, who lived through wartime rationing.

Like most of the older generation of Ambridge, Peggy still thinks of the late spring bank holiday as 'Whitsun'. But whatever you call it, a highlight of the long weekend is the annual single wicket cricket competition. The actual rules – how runs are scored, how a player gets out and so on – are the same as for any game of cricket. The key difference is that single wicket cricket is a knockout competition for individuals, not teams.

You typically start with sixteen players, who are drawn in pairs to play against each other. In the first round, let us say Rex plays against Tracy. Rex bowls an over (six balls), against Tracy batting. Then they swap round. Whoever scores the most runs in their over, or until they are out, goes through to the next round. The eight winning players go on to round two, four into the semi-finals, and the last two players battle it out in the final. In every game, ten of the other players take it in turns to do the fielding and wicket keeping.

Cricket is surely the only sport that stops for tea, and the single wicket version is no exception. After a couple of rounds, players and (unusually) spectators crowd into the Jack Woolley Pavilion and gorge themselves on sandwiches and cake. It is an ideal preparation for sitting in a deckchair for the rest of the afternoon, applauding gently. But how anyone manages to play cricket after that feast is a mystery.

CORONATION CHICKEN SANDWICHES

Serves 4

1 tbsp olive oil
1 small onion, peeled and chopped
2 tsp curry powder
150ml mayonnaise
75ml Greek yoghurt
3 tbsp mango chutney
dash of Worcestershire sauce, to taste
2 cooked chicken breasts
2 tbsp chopped coriander
2 tbsp flaked almonds, toasted
salt and black pepper

For the sandwiches
8 slices of good bread
butter
Little Gem lettuce

Heat the oil in a pan and cook the onion gently over a low
heat until softened but not browned. Stir in the curry powder
and cook for another few minutes, then tip the onion and
curry powder into a bowl. Stir in the mayonnaise, yoghurt,
chutney and Worcestershire sauce, then season with salt
and pepper.

Dice the chicken breasts and mix them with the sauce, then leave in the fridge for at least 2 hours or overnight. Before using, stir in some chopped coriander and the toasted almonds.

To make the sandwiches, butter the bread, add a good helping of coronation chicken to half the slices and top with a few lettuce leaves. Sandwich with the remaining slices of bread, then cut into halves or triangles and serve.

The cricket team started the competition in 1994, to commemorate the death of their captain in a car crash. This is why his widow Shula usually presents the Mark Hebden Memorial Trophy to the winner. Although it took until 2016 before the village team accepted women, the single wicket has always been unisex. In fact, in the inaugural match, Clarrie Grundy faced John Archer in the final round. She could have won, if Eddie hadn't dropped a catch off John's batting, and then kicked the ball over the boundary for four. Eddie swore both acts were accidental. But when it transpired that he had drawn John in an unofficial sweepstake and stood to win £30, Eddie's protestations of innocence held as much water as a woollen jerrycan.

SCONES
Makes about 12

225g plain flour, plus extra for rolling
½ tsp bicarbonate of soda
1 tsp cream of tartar
½ tsp salt
45g butter
120ml milk, plus extra for brushing

Preheat the oven to 220°C/Fan 200°C/Gas 7.

Sift the dry ingredients into a bowl, then add the butter and rub it in with your fingertips. Add the 120ml of milk and mix to form a soft dough.

Turn the dough out onto a floured surface and roll out to about 2cm thick. It's best to handle the dough as little as possible or the scones will be tough.

Cut the scones out into rounds with a pastry cutter and put them on an ungreased baking tray. Brush the tops with a little milk, then bake for about 10 minutes. Cool briefly on a wire rack, then eat warm with butter and jam.

For cheese scones, add about 85g of grated Cheddar to the dry ingredients and sprinkle a little more cheese on top of the scones before baking.

For fruit scones, add about 60g of dried fruit (currants and/or sultanas) to the mixture.

Scones freeze well. Just defrost and warm them through in the oven before serving.

Four years after Mark's death, Shula started seeing Alistair Lloyd. But when her precious son Daniel fell ill and Richard Locke proved so supportive, a sudden passion bloomed between them and they started a secret affair. Secret until it became public, that is (thank you, Susan Carter). It got ugly and Richard had to leave the village. As Mark was a solicitor, Alistair a vet and Richard a doctor, Joe Grundy observed with his customary bluntness that Borsetshire's dentists had better look out. He may have had a point. As well as being successful professionals, the men were all talented cricketers, so it seems Shula may have a 'type'.

Alistair eventually found it in himself to forgive Shula, but by 2016 the cracks were showing in their marriage. She followed her mother's rather old-fashioned suggestion that, to see more of her husband, she could help Fallon with the cricket teas. It was not a success. The teams devoured Fallon's delicacies, while Shula's rather basic offerings were barely touched. Meat paste sandwich, anyone? No, perhaps not.

LEMON DRIZZLE CAKE
Makes about 10 slices

225g butter, room temperature
225g golden caster sugar
4 eggs, lightly beaten
250g self-raising flour
grated zest of 1 unwaxed lemon

Drizzle
juice of 2 lemons
90g caster or demerara sugar

Preheat the oven to 180°C/Fan 160°C/Gas 4. Line a 900g loaf tin with greaseproof paper. Put the soft butter in a bowl with the caster sugar and beat with an electric beater until the mixture is really pale and fluffy. Beat in the eggs, one at a time, then fold in the flour and lemon zest until well combined.

Scoop the mixture into the prepared tin and smooth the top. Bake for about 50 minutes, and then check by inserting a skewer into the cake – it should come out clean.

Mix the lemon juice with the 90g sugar. Using a skewer, make holes all over the top of the warm cake, then carefully pour over the drizzle mixture and let it sink into the cake. Leave the cake to cool completely in the tin, then remove, slice and enjoy.

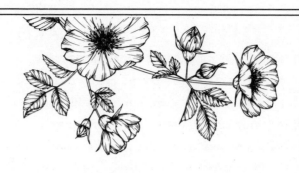

CHAPTER TEN

June

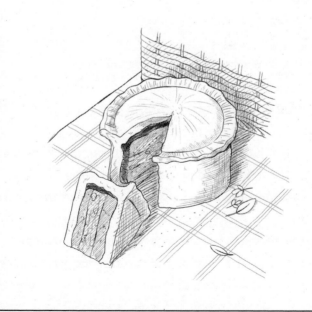

'This way! This way!' A small queue of cars has formed on the driveway into Brookfield. High-vis-jacketed, Josh is ushering them off the track into a field that was cut for silage a couple of weeks ago. Today it serves as a makeshift car park. A home-made sign by the gateway proclaims, 'Welcome to Brookfield – a Mixed Family Farm'.

LEAF (Linking Environment And Farming) invented Open Farm Sunday in 2006, and the farms of Ambridge have been taking part since 2008. The idea is to give the British public a chance to see at first hand how their food is made, and better understand what farmers do all day. Basically is it a big PR exercise, but as so few of us have any real contact with farms (unless we listen to *The Archers*, of course . . .) it is a rare opportunity to snoop behind the five-bar gate. LEAF reckons there have been over two million visits since they started the annual event.

A straggle of visitors heads up towards the yard. Retired couples, babies snoozing in papooses, small excited people held tightly by mum's hand, surly teenagers inappropriately dressed in ripped jeans and immaculate trainers . . . 'It'll be fun!' their desperate parents have promised them. Anything to drag them away from a screen for a few hours.

Expectant in the yard is a freshly washed tractor and trailer, straw bales forming rudimentary seating. Most of the 1600 or so UK farms that are open today offer some form of tour, and Brookfield is no exception. David, Ruth and Pip will take turns to motor gently around, stopping regularly to explain the key features of their home and workplace.

'Tea . . .? Coffee . . .?'

Leonard is standing behind a trestle table near the farmhouse. Seeing that the day was going to involve the whole family, he had volunteered to help out, adding quickly: 'As long as no one asks me about, I don't know, milk yields or . . .'

'EBVs?'

'Exactly, Ruth.'

Touched by the offer and grateful for any help, Jill said he was welcome to run the refreshments stall with her. They had made an early start this morning, assembling Hereford beef rolls and laying out a selection of cakes.

'. . . or how about some lemonade?'

A nine-year-old peers suspiciously at the jug in Leonard's hand, distrusting the pale cloudy liquid inside.

'That's not lemonade.'

'It is. Really.'

'Why isn't it in a bottle?'

'It's home-made. With real lemons.'

FRESH LEMONADE

5 unwaxed lemons
125g caster sugar
thin slices of lemon, to serve

Scrub 2 of the lemons really well and cut them into quarters. Juice the rest of the lemons.

Put the lemon quarters and all the juice into a food processor, add the sugar and about 200ml of water. Blitz to a purée, then tip the mixture into a large jug and top up with another litre of cold water. Stir well.

Chill and serve with ice and thin slices of lemon.

Bridge Farm has sometimes contributed to Brookfield's open day, but this year they are running their own. Anya in the shop is doing great business, while outside Helen is giving away samples of Borsetshire Blue cheese.

'Everything all right, love?'

Pat is passing with an empty tray.

'Oh . . . yes. I was just thinking.'

JUNE

Helen's notoriety as 'that woman who stabbed her husband' has faded a little, thank goodness. But she still remembers 2017, and the vultures who only turned up to press her for the gory details, and even take selfies with her. She shakes off the memory. 'Those are going well.'

'I should have made more', smiles Pat. 'There's only one batch left!'

PORK, PRUNE AND PISTACHIO PIES
Makes 8

1 tbsp olive oil
1 onion, peeled and finely chopped
2 garlic cloves, peeled and chopped
450kg pork fillet, trimmed and diced
1 leek, finely chopped
100g soft dried prunes, roughly chopped
25g pistachios, roughly chopped
1 tbsp chopped parsley
freshly grated nutmeg
650g puff pastry
flour, for dusting
1 egg, beaten, to glaze
salt and black pepper

First make the filling. Heat the oil in a frying pan, add the chopped onion and cook gently until softened and translucent.

Add the garlic and cook for a couple of minutes longer. Next, brown the pork – best to do this in a couple of batches so you don't overcrowd the pan. Once all the pork is browned, add the leek, prunes, pistachios and parsley, then season with nutmeg, salt and pepper. Set the pan aside and leave the filling to cool.

Roll out the pastry on a floured work surface and cut out 8 circles to line 8 individual flan tins or holes in a muffin tin. Cut the rest of the pastry into strips.

Preheat the oven to 180°C/Fan 160°C/Gas 4. Spoon the cool filling into the pastry cases and brush the edges with beaten egg. Arrange strips of pastry over the top of each pie to create a lattice pattern, then brush with beaten egg. Bake for 35–40 minutes until golden brown.

In the days when Helen's former husband Rob Titchener ran the 'mega dairy' at Berrow Farm, Open Farm Sunday was often a source of friction. Rob always thought he knew better than everyone, and certainly better than Justin Elliott's estate manager Charlie Thomas. Rob didn't take kindly to being told he had to hand out flyers outside a supermarket in Borchester. And as all the cows were housed indoors, he didn't think much of putting some unrealistically outside for the public to gawp at. Sadly on the day, one of them went into labour with a breech presentation. Alistair was able to save the mother, but the calf died. It was not a pretty sight, especially when plastered on an inside page of the *Borchester Echo*. It says volumes for Rob that his reaction was not sympathy for the calf or for those who witnessed its end, but vindication. He had never thought it was a good idea, he triumphantly told Helen. What a charmer . . .

Eventually Justin decided that the economics of milk production, even on this high-input-high-output model, did not provide sufficient return on investment. So with the agreement of his Borchester Land colleagues, he had the buildings at Berrow Farm repurposed as an intensive pig unit and recruited Neil Carter as general manager. There is no expectation of it opening to the public on Open Farm Sunday or any other day.

At Brookfield, the tractor and trailer has stopped at Hollowtree. Rex has led the dozen or so visitors to a horse chestnut tree. In its shade, a massive Gloucester Old Spots sow lies on her side, content and magnificent. She seems heedless of the ten stubby piglets crowding round her teats, squabbling and feeding. The crowd are entranced, although as many of them seem to be viewing the scene on their phones as are looking directly at the pigs. In the autumn, the fall of nuts from the tree will provide some extra treats. Although conkers are poisonous to humans, pigs will happily munch on them.

Nearby, a male blackbird excavates a worm from snout-turned earth and quickly air-freights it to the hedgerow. Hidden low down in the hawthorn is the nest, a rustic bowl which the female wove from grass and twigs, secured with mud and lined with finer grass. Instantly four chicks demand their food, necks craning up, more like mouths with bodies attached than the other way around.

As the dad flits away in search of the next morsel – a caterpillar this time, perhaps – Rex is explaining the benefits of outdoor-reared pigs: 'They can behave the way nature intended. They're free to snuffle and root around in the ground, make nests, interact with other pigs. They get lots of exercise, which is more expensive on feed, but great for the meat quality. It's just so much kinder than places like – well, those big pig factories.' He falls short of naming the establishment. But Pip, leaning against the big wheel of the tractor and looking on, knows he is thinking of Berrow Farm.

Ironically, just a couple of days ago Hannah Riley was in The Bull, pint in hand, fiercely defending her workplace: 'OK, yes, so we've got six thousand pigs in the fattening unit, but it's not a case of how many there are in total, it's what life's like for each individual pig. They're all on straw so they can behave naturally, and they get fresh straw like three times a week. They can eat when they want, the environment's controlled perfectly for them; they're never too hot or cold. We produce good-quality, affordable pork and we really care about our pigs. People just don't understand.' She slams the glass down on the bar for emphasis.

Phoebe Tucker stood open-mouthed, taken aback at the tirade. 'I . . . only asked how work was,' she stutters.

'Um, yeah . . . sorry. I get a bit defensive sometimes. What are you drinking?'

After Tom hooked up with Natasha, Hannah did her best to bury her heartache through a combination of hard work and hard partying. She could see how in thrall Tom was to this glamorous incomer, not just emotionally but in business matters as well. When Tom decided to do away with the Bridge Farm pigs, which his deceased brother John had started, furious Pat blamed Natasha's influence. But to be honest it did not make much difference to the customer. Rex's pigs now supply the meat, which Tom and Maurice Horton process into sausages and other products in one of the business units at Sawyers Farm. If Tom is the Tigger of Ambridge, always bouncing around from one new idea to another, Maurice is most definitely Eeyore. He is a good butcher, but he does not really do cheerful.

SAUSAGE TRAY BAKE
Serves 4

600g new potatoes, halved
1 red pepper, cut into thick strips
1 yellow pepper, cut into thick strips
2 red onions, peeled and cut into wedges
1 garlic clove, chopped
1 bay leaf
1 tsp chopped thyme leaves
½ tsp dried sage
2 tbsp olive oil
8 pork sausages
200g cherry tomatoes
salt and black pepper

Preheat the oven to 200°C/Fan 180°C/Gas 6. Put the potatoes, peppers and onions in a roasting tin and add the garlic and herbs. Drizzle with the oil, season with salt and pepper and then toss well so all the vegetables are coated in oil and seasoning.

Put the roasting tin in the oven for about 20 minutes. Remove, place the sausages on top of the vegetables and nestle the tomatoes around them. Spoon some of the juices from the tin over the sausages.

Put the tin back in the oven and roast for 25–30 minutes or until the sausages are golden-brown and cooked through. Serve with some green vegetables or salad.

Back at Brookfield, the trailer has moved on. By now the visitors are starting to realise that grass is not something which just grows; it is a vital crop which needs careful management.

'So this is one of the fields we'll be hoping to cut for hay in a few weeks.' Pip cocks an eye at the sky, and the glowering clouds that today threaten a sharp shower. 'As long as the weather co-operates.'

'Make hay while the sun shines,' observes a trim pensioner, plump-lensed camera prominent on his chest.

'Exactly. And we need nearly a week of it.'

'Good luck with that.'

Although Pip is hoping to get the job done by the end of the month, haymaking is so dependent on good weather that sometimes it has to be left as late as August. It starts in a similar way to silage-making: they cut the grass and leave it to wilt. But then it is turned in the field every day for three to five days, so that the sun dries it before baling. Farmers' stress levels are often pretty high, but they can go off the scale during these critical few days. Even slightly damp hay can go mouldy. Or even worse, the bales can start to heat up and burst into flames. And if the hay gets wet and then dries before baling, it can become dusty and cause breathing problems for both animals and people. The 'farmer's lung' cited for years by Joe Grundy is not an excuse to avoid work, but a real disease caused by a reaction to the spores in mouldy hay. Well, all right, in Joe's case it may sometimes have been an excuse to avoid work . . .

JUNE

Behind the Scenes

The Archers scripts are written up to three months ahead of transmission and recorded a good month ahead. We have a comprehensive advance diary system which flags up holidays, major sporting events and the like. But no one can accurately predict the weather that far ahead. This is why Ambridge may sometimes enjoy hay-perfect sunshine, while the nation shelters from unseasonal storms. Of course, when by chance we get it right, no one notices . . .

Brookfield makes both big round bales and smaller rectangular bales – the classic size and shape that most people picture as a hay or straw bale. Big bales are easier to handle with a tractor and less labour-intensive at haymaking time. But the smaller bales can be taken out to the field on the rack of a quad bike or chucked into the back of a 4x4. Although silage packs more nutritional punch, hay is still a useful feedstuff for sheep and horses.

The meadow hay that Ed Grundy makes at Grange Farm is important for two reasons. He needs it to feed his Texel sheep through the winter, and he sells the surplus at a sizeable profit to horse-owning types like Lavinia Rafferty. Ed makes his small bales, and Brookfield's, with a vintage piece of kit called a Jones Baler. Oliver Sterling kindly passed it on free of charge in 2009, when Ed started to rent Grange Farm's fifty acres. It was just one of Oliver's many generous acts, which have supported Ed's uneven progress as a farmer.

◇◇◇◇◇◇◇◇◇◇◇◇◇◇◇◇◇◇◇◇◇◇◇◇◇◇◇◇◇◇◇◇◇◇◇◇◇◇◇

Ambridge International

ITALY

◇◇◇◇◇◇◇◇◇◇◇◇◇◇◇◇◇◇◇◇◇◇◇◇◇◇◇◇◇◇◇◇◇◇◇◇◇◇◇

Oliver Sterling and Caroline Pemberton discovered a mutual love of Italian opera in 2002. Soon after, they joined a local Italian society and began to learn the language. When their teacher Cosima started to flirt with Oliver, Caroline became jealous. But she quickly realised that it showed how much she cared about him.

They married in 2006 and after ten blissful years cemented their Italian love affair by buying a villa in Tuscany. But their plans for a sun-drenched retirement were ended by Caroline's sudden death there in July 2017. It nearly broke poor Oliver. On Christmas morning, Roy Tucker found him cloistered in his room at Grey Gables. He was listening to an anguished aria from Puccini's *Tosca*: 'E lucevan le stelle' ('the stars were shining'), in which a condemned man remembers the woman he loved, and whom he will never see again.

It was probably Oliver's lowest moment. He gradually

came to find a way of living without Caroline, even working part-time at The Bull for a while. He is a decent fellow, an old-school gentleman, and no one says 'splendid' quite like him.

ASPARAGUS PASTA
Serves 4

300g asparagus
1 tbsp olive oil
1 garlic clove, halved
1 strip of pared lemon zest
400g tagliatelle
1 egg yolk
75ml crème fraiche or double cream
50g Parmesan cheese, grated, plus extra for serving
handful of basil leaves
salt and black pepper

First prepare the asparagus. Bend the spears to breaking point and snap off the woody ends (save them for soup, if you like). Slice off the tips and slice the remaining stems thinly on the diagonal. Set aside.

Heat the olive oil in a large sauté pan. Add the garlic halves and cook until the garlic is close to changing colour, then remove it and add the asparagus and lemon zest. Continue to cook the asparagus until just cooked – it should still have some bite.

Meanwhile, bring a large pot of water to the boil and add plenty of salt. Add the pasta and cook until just al dente. Strain, reserving a ladleful of the cooking liquid, and add the drained pasta to the sauté pan. Remove the pan from the heat. Whisk the egg yolk with the crème fraiche or double cream and pour this over the pasta. Sprinkle in the grated Parmesan and season with salt and pepper. Using a couple of forks, mix to combine by pulling the strands up. Add some of the reserved cooking water if the sauce seems too thick.

Remove the lemon zest from the pan, then add the basil leaves and let them wilt. Serve immediately with more Parmesan cheese.

At Brookfield, the tour has reached the dairy herd. The multi-patterned cows graze peacefully in the midday quiet. No longer needing to find a mate, the birds have piped down as summer has come into full bloom.

'Aren't they a bit squashed together?'

Pip addresses the questioner, a keen-eyed woman with purple hair and a T-shirt to match.

'I thought someone might say that.' The cows are indeed at a greater density than the casual walker or driver might be used to seeing. 'You're probably wondering why they're only in one half of the field.'

Pip explains the principle. Rather than let the herd graze randomly in the fields, they have divided them into paddocks with a combination of semi-permanent fencing and electric wire. Right now, the cows are tucking into a rich mixture of grass, herbs and clovers. When they come back from milking tomorrow morning, Pip will move the electric fences to give them access to the next area, and to close the one behind. By the time the herd returns, this paddock will have had weeks to recover and regenerate into another nutrient-packed smorgasbord. This enables Brookfield to leave their cows outside for many months, keeping their costs down, their animals healthy, and their milk quality high.

'If you really want to see cattle close together, you should see a mob grazing system. They do that over at Home Farm with beef cattle on herbal leys—'

'Home Farm? Are they the ones that do the strawber-ries?'

In previous years, when not opening their own doors to the public, Adam and Jennifer had brought their farmers' market stall to Brookfield, and done a brisk trade.

'They used to, but they've stopped that now. They're raising fish instead.'

'Fish?'

'Yes.'

'How am I going to make jam out of fish?'

STRAWBERRY JAM
Makes about 4 jars

1kg redcurrants
1.8kg strawberries
1.8kg preserving sugar

First make the redcurrant juice. Wash the redcurrants and put them in a pan with a small amount of water. Cook gently until soft, then tip them into a muslin-lined sieve over a bowl and press to extract the juice. Set the juice aside. Put a couple of saucers in the freezer for checking the set later.

Wash and hull the strawberries and put them in a large pan with the sugar. Heat gently until the sugar has dissolved. Add 240ml of the redcurrant juice, bring to the boil and boil rapidly for 10–15 minutes, then test for setting. Put a small amount of jam on one of the cold saucers and push it with your finger. If it wrinkles, the jam is ready. If not, boil it for a few more minutes.

When the setting point has been reached, remove the pan from the heat and set it aside for about 20 minutes, before pouring the jam into warm sterilised jars. Cover with lids or jam-pot covers and store in a cool, dark place. Once opened, store jars in the fridge.

'So what did you say?'

'What could I say?'

The final car has disappeared up the track. As Ruth brings in the cows, Pip and Ben are dismantling the information board by the milking parlour.

'OK, Pip, you win.'

'Win?'

'That was definitely the weirdest question today. Even weirder than "Do brown cows give chocolate milk?".'

Ruth pauses nearby, as the herd streams into the collecting yard: 'Well done, you two.'

'Are you sure you're OK to do the milking, Mum?'

'Absolutely, pet. Have either of you eaten yet?

'Haven't really had the time.'

'Ben?'

'Bar of chocolate.'

'OK. Leave that for a bit, then. Gran's got something for you in the kitchen. It'll keep you going until your tea.'

'Mum . . .?'

'What, love?'

'How do you make jam from fish?'

Ruth blinks. 'I'm sorry?'

WATERCRESS SOUP
Serves 4

2 big bunches of watercress
2 tbsp butter
1 large onion, peeled and finely chopped
1 large floury potato, peeled and diced
1 celery stick, chopped
800ml chicken or vegetable stock
150ml double cream, plus extra to serve
freshly grated nutmeg
salt and black pepper

Wash the watercress well, then pick it over, discarding any damaged or dead leaves. Chop up most of the watercress, reserving a few of the best leaves and sprigs for garnishing the soup.

Melt the butter in a large pan, add the onion and cook it gently until softened. Add the potato and celery and continue to cook for another 5 minutes. Do not allow the vegetables to brown. Add the chopped watercress and the stock and bring them to the boil. Turn the heat down to a simmer and cook for another 20 minutes.

Take the pan off the heat and leave to cool a little, then blitz the soup in a blender or with a stick blender. Add the cream, season with salt and pepper and a little nutmeg, then gently warm through. Serve garnished with a few reserved watercress leaves and a little swirl of cream.

'Yes! I've got – ooh . . .' As a breadcrumb catches in his throat, Ben's triumphant cry becomes a fusillade of coughing. David pounds him firmly on the back.

'Are you all right? You've got what?'

Still croaky, Ben manages to get out the words. 'How do you make jam from fish? You get a jar and fillet!'

The family groans. Across the table, Josh lowers his soup spoon and raises an eyebrow.

'Dad . . . you should have let him choke.'

CHAPTER ELEVEN

July

We expect a lot of July. It should be the height of summer, and the school holidays are starting, so why is it raining, for Pete's sake? In fact, rain falls somewhere in England on an average of ten to fourteen days in July. Not much fun if you are at the seaside. But for farmers, a drought is bad news indeed. So when you next gaze bleakly at a grey beach through the rivulets running down a rain-dashed windowpane, you can console yourself with the very British thought that at least it is good for the grass.

No beach break for the farmer right now. The arable harvest will start in the middle of the month. So in preparation for this hectic and crucial period, there is much checking of equipment, greasing of trailers, pumping of tyres and sweeping out of grain stores.

Tom at Bridge Farm needs to prepare for his small arable harvest, but at the same time the work on the vegetable crops is relentless. This is a time of peak production – peak weed production too – and as an organic farmer he cannot resort to chemical controls. The weeds in some crops, such as cabbages, can be kept down with a three-bladed hoe towed behind a tractor. But for carrots, Tom needs to lie down on the job – or preferably persuade some other people to.

A few wisps of high cirrus cloud do nothing to moderate the heat of the sun toasting the backs of Tom's helpers. They are lying face down and side by side on a wheeled contraption called a lazy weeder. But there is nothing lazy about this job. The tractor pulls the prone workers slowly through the field, but their hands move constantly, picking out the unwanted plants from between the feathery green carrot tops. Elsewhere, the bright blue irrigation pipes must be moved regularly, and a host of vegetables and salad crops, both in and out of the polytunnels, need harvesting and thinning out.

Much of this produce will find its way into the veg boxes. Pat and Tony set up their box scheme in 1994, and for more than twenty years it ran on classic lines. In this system, customers pay a regular weekly sum, choosing the price level that suits them. Every week they have a box delivered to their door, containing a mixture of whatever is in season. What they sacrifice in choice, they make up for in convenience, freshness and the satisfaction of knowing that they are supporting a local family-run, eco-friendly enterprise. A weekly newsletter gives updates from the farm, and recipe suggestions for that week's offerings.

Then along came Hurricane Natasha, shaking Tom to his wellies. He had been doing his best to make the boxes as interesting as possible, with lines like pak choi, golden beetroot and heritage tomatoes, but their loyal customers were almost all middle-aged and older. Natasha's SWOT analysis saw in this situation not Strength, but Weakness and Threat – and so Opportunity.

As she explained to the bank's 'relationship manager': 'People expect choice. Your Millennials and Generation Zeds, they're used to picking from everything in the world and having it today. Fancy a turmeric latte and a cronut?

Get it Deliveroo'd.'

'Cronut . . .?'

'It's like a cross between a croissant and a doughnut. It's lush.'

Tom leapt in. 'Not that we're planning to sell cronuts. It's just an example.'

What they were planning was to offer their customers the same level of choice as the national market leaders. With their Bridge Fresh app and website, customers can not only tailor the contents of their box, but add almost anything from the Bridge Farm shop as well, from grains to meat and dairy products.

Pat and Tony could see the possibilities. But Tony worried about being left with surplus produce if customers started to reject less exciting items. And they were very uneasy that Tom and Natasha had set the portal up as their joint business, not a Bridge Farm one.

AGRETTI AND HERITAGE TOMATO SALAD

Serves 4

1 small red onion, finely
  sliced
1 tbsp olive oil
1 garlic clove, cut in half
1 bunch of agretti,
  trimmed and well
  washed
1 tsp lemon zest
300g heritage tomatoes
150g cooked farro
  (50g uncooked)
a selection of fresh herbs
  or micro herbs, to garnish

Dressing
pinch of saffron, soaked in
  2 tbsp warm water
100ml plain yoghurt
2 tbsp olive oil
1 tbsp lemon juice
½ tsp honey
½ garlic clove, crushed or
  grated
salt and black pepper

Soak the onion slices in ice-cold salty water for 30 minutes.

For the salad dressing, whisk all the ingredients together, including the saffron soaking water, and season with salt and pepper. Taste and adjust the acidity or sweetness as you like by adding more lemon juice or honey. If the dressing seems very thick, add a splash of water.

Next, prepare the agretti. Heat the olive oil in a large sauté pan and add the garlic halves. Fry them gently for a minute, then remove. Add the agretti and sauté for a couple of minutes, then remove the pan from the heat. Stir in the lemon zest.

Cut the tomatoes into uneven slices and chunks and sprinkle them with salt. Arrange the agretti over a large platter, then sprinkle with the farro, the drained red onions and the tomatoes.

Drizzle over a couple of tablespoons of the dressing, leaving the rest to serve at the table. Garnish with the herbs.

For now, Pat has put her worries about her son and daughter-in-law to one side. Scoop in hand, she is assembling a double waffle cone for Neville Booth.

'Lovely day for it.'

Neville does not reply, simply handing over the correct change.

'Like to try a sample of Borsetshire Blue?'

Neville shakes his head at Helen. Attacking the ice cream, and ignoring Tom's proffered Bridge Fresh flyer, he heads off towards the Extreme Eating tent.

Bridge Farm is out in force at the Lower Loxley Food Festival. The stall is packed with a selection of their most profitable items, and in the afternoon heat their ice cream stand is doing great business.

PEACH ICE CREAM
Serves 8

6 ripe peaches
3 free-range eggs
300g golden caster sugar
200g single cream
500ml double cream
¼ tsp salt
extra peaches, to serve

First peel the peaches. Score a cross in the base of each peach
with a sharp knife. Put them in a heatproof bowl and pour
over just-boiled water to cover and leave for a moment or so.
Drain and leave until cool enough to handle, then slip off the
skins.

Cut the peaches in half and remove the stones, then put the
peach flesh in a food processor and blitz to form a purée.

Beat the eggs and sugar in a bowl until pale, then add the
puréed peaches. Add the single and double creams and the salt,
then mix well until combined. Pour into an ice-cream maker
and churn until frozen. Serve with sliced fresh peaches.
Note: this recipe contains raw eggs.

Toby is taking time away from the Designer Drinks tent.
He has been doing his best to promote Scruff gin, but as
one of seven artisan spirits producers on site today he is

wondering if the market is getting saturated. He needs to diversify.

'What do you think about Scruff gin-flavoured ice cream, Pat?'

Pat does not look up from the tub of blackcurrant ripple. 'Is it organic?'

'Organic-ish . . . I mean, it's made from natural materials.'

'Sorry, Toby.'

Back in Ambridge, Rex would kill for an ice cream. The summer heat, so welcomed by the crowds at Lower Loxley, means more work for him. The sows are his engines of production, but the piglets they produce are his stock in trade. Pigs can easily get heat stress, so right now Rex is going around with a hose, refilling the wallows. These purpose-built mini ponds allow his pigs to enjoy a cooling mudbath whenever they want. A sow takes her time but eventually makes way for a group of piglets, playful as kids at a paddling pool. She lumbers off, skin coated with natural sunblock, and flops down inside her ark.

'Do you want to take a look around, Helen?'

'Hm?' Helen has been gazing vaguely into the middle distance, with an expression that her mother recognises. She saw it last month at Open Farm Sunday.

'We can cover here, can't we, Tom?'

'Uh . . . yeah, sure.'

'Go on, check out the competition.'

'All right.' Helen neatly folds her apron and wanders off to the deli tent.

You can forgive Helen for her distraction, as she was at the heart of one of the most dramatic series of events ever to happen in Ambridge. When you have been through the sort of trauma that she experienced, you may move on, but it never completely leaves you. You can be trotting along with your life, when suddenly a trigger will come out of nowhere, sparking a disturbing reprise of images, conversations, emotions . . .

Rob Titchener exercised control over Helen in every sphere of life: what she wore, who she met, even what they ate. In February 2014, he had not yet shown his true colours. Handsome, successful, considerate; he appeared to be a perfect catch. Happy Helen spent several hours cooking a special meal for them. But as soon as Rob entered the kitchen he gagged. Was she cooking tuna? He could not stand even the smell of it.

Rob was rather fussy about his desserts too, particularly when it came to custard. He had no truck with the stuff made from powder, and woe betide Helen if she brought a tin or carton of ready-made into Blossom Hill Cottage. For Rob, the only acceptable custard was one made from scratch.

PROPER CUSTARD

Serves 6

600ml whole milk
vanilla pod, split
6 egg yolks
75g sugar

Put the milk in a pan with the split vanilla pod. Heat gently and when the milk is almost at boiling point, remove the pan from the heat and set it aside for a while so the milk can infuse with the vanilla.

Whisk the egg yolks and sugar together in a bowl until they are pale and creamy. Remove the vanilla pod from the milk, then slowly strain the milk through a sieve into the egg and sugar mixture, whisking constantly. Pour the mixture back into the pan and cook gently over a low heat, stirring constantly until thickened. Do not allow it to boil. When ready, the custard should coat the back of a wooden spoon. Great served with rhubarb crumble (see page 165).

Although whether this was what Rob really thought, or whether it was just another way to control Helen, is debatable. There is no doubt that it is a scrumptious sauce, but that constant stirring makes it quite labour-intensive. For Helen to suddenly have to conjure it up, in addition to a full meal and with a small child to manage as well, could only add to her stress.

On 4 April 2016, Rob insisted on it again, not realising that Helen intended this dinner to be their final one together. Realising at last how much Rob had manipulated her, Helen had resolved to leave, taking little Henry with her. But the tuna-rich main course she set in front of Rob was a trap. As he wolfed it down, he denied ever saying he disliked the fish. It was just another example of him trying to keep the ground shifting under her. As Helen prepared the dessert, she knew for sure that he was lying. Pretty soon, the custard was on the kitchen floor, and so was Rob. He would gaslight her no longer.

Behind the Scenes

When we were planning and writing Helen and Rob's story, we worked closely with the charities Refuge and Women's Aid. Thinking of all the real Helens in abusive relationships, *Archers* listener Paul Trueman set up a JustGiving page, hoping it might raise a few thousand pounds for Refuge. After seven months, the total stood at over £170,000.

'That was quick.' Tom steps aside as Helen stows a foil bag in the cool box.

'Bought something nice?' inquires Pat.

Helen straightens up. 'Will Dad have any food for us when we get home, do you think?'

Pat pulls a face. 'I think he'll have been too busy with Jack and Henry.'

'I'll cook tonight, then.'

'All right. Thank you.'

At Grange Farm, Clarrie Grundy is cooking for the family too, although there is nothing unusual about that. If her husband even knows how to turn the oven on, he keeps very quiet about it. Today Eddie has been doing a landscaping job for a small-scale poultry farmer in Penny Hassett. He arrived home earlier, cash in one hand and a basket of eggs in the other. 'Call it a tip,' the farmer had said. So Clarrie thought she would do a version of her winning entry from the 2018 Flower and Produce Show. Although Jennifer Aldridge scooped the Freda Fry Memorial Trophy for overall achievement, this particular dish had beaten Jennifer's similar offering into second place. But despite its illustrious history, Clarrie never told Joe its proper name, knowing that he was always suspicious of anything resembling 'foreign muck'. So this is an omelette, all right?

VEGETABLE FRITTATA
Serves 4

150g fresh peas
1 tbsp olive oil
4 spring onions, trimmed and chopped
1 garlic clove, peeled and chopped
1 courgette, diced
6 eggs
handful of basil leaves, torn
handful of rocket, roughly chopped
50g Cheddar cheese, grated
salt and black pepper

Bring a pan of salted water to the boil and cook the peas until tender. Drain, refresh under cold water and set them aside. Preheat the grill.

Heat the olive oil in a frying pan, add the chopped spring onions and garlic. Fry them until softened but not browned, then add the diced courgette and cook until softened.

Meanwhile, beat the eggs in a bowl and add the basil and rocket and the cheese. Season with salt and pepper. Pour the egg mixture over the vegetables in the pan and cook for a few minutes over a medium heat until the underside is set. Put the pan under the hot grill for a few moments to finish cooking and brown the top. Serve cut into wedges with a green salad.

✦✦✦

Ambridge International

FRANCE

✦✦✦

In 1992, when the Grundys were struggling to make a go of Grange Farm, Clarrie had an idea. At the time, some British farmers were relocating across the channel, taking advantage of the much lower French land prices. Eddie agreed to an exploratory visit, but when he discovered they would have to pay for their travel and accommodation, he decided they should camp. They set off with hope in their hearts and a borrowed tent. Unfortunately, Eddie was sick on the ferry, the airbed leaked, and the van broke down on the Champs-Élysées.

Buying a farm was also a non-starter, but Clarrie returned with a *grande passion* for all things French. She was a prime mover in getting Ambridge twinned with the village of Meyruelle and was part of the first delegation to visit. She also became friends with Grey Gables' head chef Jean-Paul. It was perfectly innocent, but jealous Eddie misinterpreted their *entente cordiale*, and punched the blameless chef on the nose. Clarrie was mortified.

CHERRY CLAFOUTIS

Serves 6

butter, for greasing
500g cherries, pitted
2 tbsp golden caster sugar
1 tbsp Kirsch (optional)

Batter
3 eggs
60g golden caster sugar
30g plain flour
350ml whole milk
25g butter, melted
icing sugar, to serve

Preheat the oven to 180°C/Fan 160°C/Gas 4.

Butter a flan dish, spread the cherries over the base and sprinkle them with the sugar and the Kirsch, if using.

To make the batter, beat the eggs and sugar in a bowl, then sift in the flour and mix. Whisk in the milk and melted butter and then pour the mixture over the cherries. Bake for about 30 minutes until puffed up and golden brown. Sprinkle with the icing sugar and serve warm with cream or crème fraiche.

Clafoutis can be made with other fruits, although then it is more properly called *flaugnarde* (meaning 'soft'). But this classic recipe with cherries is particularly appropriate now, because at Home Farm the trees in the polytunnels are laden with the luscious, rich red fruit. Adam checks that they are 'tree-ripe' – sweet-tasting and dark-fleshed – and confirms it by testing the sugar content of the juice. Cherries are one of the most perishable and easily damaged soft fruits, so the pickers handle them delicately, lay them in shallow containers and get them into refrigeration as quickly as possible.

When not supervising cherry operations, Adam walks his crops, assessing when they will be ready to cut. First under the combine harvester will be the winter wheat, which he sowed last September. He stoops to snap an ear from a stalk which has lost almost all of its green colour. Once it becomes fully straw-like, no more nutrition will be reaching the head, which will start to slowly decline in quality. The trick is to catch it at just the right moment. Adam pulls out a single grain and digs his thumbnail in. Not yet; a couple of weeks, maybe. He moves on to a field of maize. The plants are up to his knees now, but the familiar green leaf-wrapped torpedoes are not yet developed. It will be October before this crop is ready for harvest. And the quinoa in the next field will have to wait until the leaves have dropped and the seeds dried in September. Of course, the fate of this fashionable grain is a matter of supreme indifference to Jazzer. Give him chips any day.

QUINOA, ROCKET AND RED PEPPER SALAD

Serves 4

100g quinoa
200ml vegetable stock
2 red peppers
25g pine nuts, toasted
150g feta cheese, cut into cubes
2 tbsp olive oil
juice of 1 lemon
good handful of rocket leaves
salt and black pepper

Rinse the quinoa in a sieve and tip it into a pan. Add the hot stock, bring it to the boil and cook for 10–15 minutes until the quinoa is tender and the water has been absorbed. Set aside.

Meanwhile, cut the peppers in half and remove the seeds. Place them cut-side down on a grill pan and grill until the skins are charred and blackened. Transfer them to a bowl, cover with a lid and leave them to steam for 15 minutes. When they're cool enough to handle, peel off the skins and discard. Cut the peppers into strips.

Put the quinoa in a bowl and add the strips of pepper, pine nuts and cubes of feta. Add the olive oil and lemon juice, season with salt and pepper and mix gently to combine. Stir in the rocket leaves and serve at once.

Half a mile away in Lyttleton Covert, Pete closes the gate of a large pen, the wire netting taller than him. He opens the lid from the plastic crate he has just brought in, and lifts out the latest pheasant poults that he has been raising. Six weeks old and about half their fully grown size, they are gawky things, mottled brown with stubby tails. The youngsters start to investigate their new home, well provisioned with food, water, shrubby undergrowth to scratch in, and some felled tree branches to perch on. Pete observes them with pride. These birds will stay in this 'release pen' for a month or so, getting used to living outdoors and growing in size and confidence. Their tails will lengthen and the cock birds will develop their iridescent red, white and blue head colouring.

Foxes are their greatest danger during this time. The pen is surrounded by an electric fence, and the wire netting walls are dug 30cm into the earth to deter burrowing. Despite these fortifications, Pete may be out tonight with a high-powered lamp and rifle.

The Archers have returned to Bridge Farm, pleased with their busy day.

'Are you sure I can't help?' Sitting at the dining table as instructed, Pat is uncomfortable about being waited on.

'It's fine,' Helen calls. 'It's done now, anyway.'

'I must say I'm ready for this.' After a day in the company of two rumbustious boys, Tony has a weary look and a mighty appetite.

Helen approaches the table, a steaming gratin dish clasped in a tea towel. Pat moves a plate of wholemeal sourdough to make space. 'It smells delicious.'

'Good.' Helen carefully places the dish down. 'It's something I . . . well, I haven't made it for ages. I thought it was about time I did.'

TUNA BAKE
Serves 4

400g any type of short pasta – penne, fusilli, etc.
600ml milk
1 bay leaf
30g butter
1 onion, peeled and finely chopped
2 garlic cloves, crushed
30g plain flour
2 tsp Dijon mustard
250g Cheddar cheese, grated
2 x 150g cans of tuna in spring water, drained
250g sweetcorn kernels
salt and black pepper

Preheat the oven to 200°C/Fan 180°C/Gas 6.

Bring a large pot of water to the boil. Cook the pasta to the point that it is still on the firm side of al dente, then drain.

Meanwhile, heat the milk in a pan with the bay leaf until almost boiling. Remove the pan from the heat and leave to stand. Melt the butter in a large ovenproof casserole dish, then add the onion. Sauté until the onion is very soft, then add the garlic. Cook for a further minute, then add the flour.

Stir until the flour is well combined with the butter and onion and cook for 3–4 minutes, stirring constantly, just to cook out the raw flour taste. Start adding the milk, a little at a time, stirring thoroughly to combine into a sauce. When you have added all the milk, stir in the mustard and 150g of the cheese. Stir until the cheese has melted, then add the tuna, sweetcorn and pasta. Season with salt and pepper to taste.

Sprinkle over the remaining cheese, then transfer to the oven and bake for about 20 minutes until the cheese has melted and started to brown in patches.

CHAPTER TWELVE

August

Welcome to the end – and to a host of beginnings and middles too, because the farming year is really the farming cycle. But for our arable farmers, mid-July to mid-August is the big finish; the culmination of twelve months second-guessing the weather, fighting pests and diseases, early starts and lonely tractor-bound days. No matter how much they have done correctly up to now, a thunderstorm or machinery failure at harvest time can have a real effect on their profit for the year.

For several weeks, you will not see Adam much at The Bull, or even on the cricket field. On his shoulders rests the responsibility of harvesting over 2,000 acres of crops; at Home Farm, the Berrow Estate, Brookfield and other local farms. The key piece of kit is his giant combine harvester, so called because it performs three major jobs. It reaps – cuts and gathers the crop; threshes – removes the grain or edible part; and winnows – separates the valuable grain from the inedible chaff.

It only takes one person to drive a combine, but tractors and trailers are needed to transport the grain to the farmyard. As with silage making, there is no stopping. The tractor drives alongside, and the combine operator directs the grain through a chute into the trailer.

'What's it coming in at, Brian?'

Having failed to get Adam on the mobile, David has popped over to Home Farm, desperate to know when

Adam will be able to start on his crops. David is all too aware that Brookfield's acreage is a small proportion of the total harvest, and inevitably lower in Adam's priorities.

Brian holds up a chunky hand-held device.

'Seventeen point five.'

That is the percentage moisture content of the grain. It does not meet the buyer's specification, so they will have to dry it using expensive fossil fuels. It is all part of the juggling act of harvest: wait a little longer to let the sun help out, but risk falling behind? Adam has decided to press ahead.

'Mind out.' Brian gently pulls David to one side as the latest load arrives. In the tractor cab, general farmworker Andy pulls a lever, and the bright red trailer slowly tips up. Golden grain gushes from the tailgate, adding to the head-height heap in the temporary store.

'It's coming off the combine faster than the drier can cope.'

David has been polite for long enough. 'Sure, look, which field is Adam in? I could do with a word.'

◇◇

Ambridge International

GUERNSEY

◇◇

The Berrow Estate, which to David's annoyance is taking precedence at harvest time, used to be called the Bellamy Estate. In the 1980s, it was owned by Adam's favourite auntie (everyone's favourite auntie, surely). Lilian had inherited it, and much more, on the death of her second husband Ralph Bellamy.

Despite an age gap of twenty-two years, their early married life was blissful. Ralph supported Lilian as she built up her riding stables – the establishment which Shula now owns. But after a heart scare, Ralph decided he needed a quieter life, so the couple moved to Guernsey. It was a disastrous mistake. Bored Lilian started drinking and the marriage deteriorated.

For the next twenty years, Lilian was living proof that although money could buy an awful lot of gin, it did not buy happiness. In 2001, she erupted back into the village with an actor/model toyboy in tow. Although Scott did not last long, Lilian realised that she would be much happier back on home turf.

Ambridge would never be the same again.

GUERNSEY GÂCHE

Makes 1 small loaf

450g plain flour, plus extra for rolling
2 tbsp caster sugar
1 tsp salt
7g instant dried yeast
225g butter (Guernsey for preference), plus extra for
  greasing
350g sultanas
50g mixed peel
240ml warm milk

Put the flour, sugar, salt and yeast in a bowl, then rub in the butter with your fingertips. Stir in the sultanas and mixed peel, then pour in the milk and mix to a soft dough. Turn the dough out onto a floured surface and knead to make sure the fruit is mixed through evenly. Put the dough back in the bowl, cover with cling film or a damp tea towel and leave to rise in a warm place for about 2 hours.

Preheat the oven to 220°C/Fan 200°C/Gas 7. Grease a 450g loaf tin with butter. Shape the dough into a loaf, put it in the tin and bake for 30 minutes. Turn the oven down to 200°C/180°C/Gas 6 and bake for another 30 minutes. Remove from the oven and leave to cool in the tin for 15 minutes, then turn out onto a wire rack to cool completely. Serve as it is, spread with Guernsey butter or toasted.

AUGUST

In the orchard at Brookfield, two anonymous figures work carefully. White-clad and face-veiled, they look like cricket umpires on a mission to Mars.

'Before you take the super off, I'll give them some smoke, shall I?'

'Thanks, Gran.'

When Adam eventually gets over to Brookfield, Josh will be needed for grain hauling. But at the moment he has a little time, so he has asked Jill if she would like to help extract the last of this year's honey. The beehive is a construction of stacked wooden boxes. Josh has prised the top one – the super – from the one below it, breaking the wax seal that the bees have made.

'Nowadays a full one's a bit heavy for me, I'm afraid.'

'No problem,' Josh assures her.

Working the bellows of the smoker, Jill directs a couple of puffs into the top of the super. The smoke has two effects. It masks the bees' alarm pheromone, and also triggers an instinctive response to return to the hive and feed. It makes them much safer to work around. Josh easily lifts off the super, places it on the ground, and draws out one of the ten vertical wooden frames.

'Not bad.'

Most of the honeycomb-mesh of the frame is covered with wax. They know that underneath this capping they will find the honey they are seeking.

'That's a relief,' says Jill.

Josh took on the hives in 2016. But having nursed the bees for nearly thirty years, through full and lean years, colony collapse and attacks from the notorious Varroa mite, Jill still takes a close interest in them.

'There should be plenty for your baking.'

'Thank you.'

As usual, Jill has pledged a substantial contribution for the WI stall at the Ambridge Summer Fete.

HONEY FLAPJACKS
Makes 16

100g unsalted butter, plus extra for greasing
4 tbsp runny honey
100g soft brown sugar
180g porridge oats
30g sultanas

Preheat the oven to 170°C/Fan 150°C/Gas 3½ and grease a 20cm square baking tin with butter. Put the butter, honey and sugar in a pan and heat very gently until everything has melted and combined.

Put the oats and sultanas in a bowl, then pour in the butter and honey mixture and mix well. Tip the mixture into the greased tin and press it down well. Bake for about 20 minutes until golden, then set aside to cool in the tin. Don't try to turn it out, as the mixture will be quite soft until it has cooled. Once it is cold, cut the flapjacks into squares. Store in an airtight tin.

'You'll have to promise me one thing though, Gran.'

As he replaces the lid on the hive, Josh's smile can he heard rather than seen.

'What's that?'

'They'd better not be used as offensive weapons. I don't want to be aiding and abetting a criminal.'

Jill is smiling too. 'No, I think I've learned my lesson.'

An unlikely combination of the bees and the WI are part of the reason that pillar-of-the-community Jill has a criminal record. In 2017, Kirsty encouraged her to attend a talk by Patrick Hennessey from Borsetshire Wildlife Trust. Inspired, Jill helped out at a BWT stall, talking about the environmental threat to pollinators such as bees. She went on to volunteer at a social enterprise, the Happy Friends Café. This pay-what-you-can place cooked meals with donated food which would otherwise be wasted, but it was being forced out of its easily accessible site in the centre of Borchester. To add insult to injury, it was to be replaced with a high-end restaurant. Les Soeurs Heureuses was the latest venture from the notoriously arrogant and extravagant Lulu and Miriam Duxford.

Jill's sense of natural justice was outraged. On 25 July, she was part of a demonstration outside the new restaurant, protesting against food waste. Being Jill, naturally she had brought snacks for everyone. But when it seemed the protestors would not be allowed to put their point across, Jill saw red. She let fly with the flapjack that was in her hand, and soon everyone was bombarding the sisters with baked goods. PC Harrison Burns had no option but to arrest Jill. She received a police caution, and (almost as embarrassing) had to concede the irony of throwing food to protest against food waste.

Behind the Scenes

Flapjackgate coincided with Patricia Greene's sixtieth anniversary playing Jill when 'Paddy', as she is known, was eighty-six years old. We are honoured to work with talented actors who still deliver excellent performances long after most occupations would have waved them off into retirement.

The standard-bearer of our many valiant seniors is undoubtedly June Spencer, who debuted as Peggy (then Archer) in our very first episode on 1 January 1951. In June 2019, Peggy energised and alarmed the family by announcing that she wanted to invest a large sum in a new and innovative environmental project. Listeners to the episode could not have guessed that the actor behind that dominant performance was one hundred years old.

One of the ways in which Kirsty had inspired Jill's renewed interest in the environment had been to show her the herbal leys at Home Farm. Jill was overwhelmed at the profusion of shapes and colours. In all his hectic harvest schedule, Adam has to remember to move his beef cattle on to the next area of the leys for some 'fresh bite', or to get someone else to do it. Despite the feeling of high summer, the grasses and other species are slowing their growth now, so this is a daily job. And at Brookfield, Pip is making the paddocks progressively larger to make sure the cows get sufficient nourishment. Even so, the milk yields are dropping from their annual high point in June. It does make milking a quicker task, though.

'So when do you think, Adam?'

David has hitched a tractor ride back out to the field and flagged down the combine. The machine towers over them. Ahead are the upright golden stalks which will soon yield their riches. Behind, untidy rows of chopped straw and chaff.

Adam assumes an expression not unlike a builder about to quote on a job. 'Thursday, maybe?'

'Really? It's ready now.'

'Yeah, but the forecast's looking OK. You can wait a few days, surely.'

As the men haggle, wood pigeons and rooks scavenge for spilt grain among the stubble. This is a time of plenty for them, too.

Meanwhile, in an outhouse at Brookfield, Josh is scraping the wax capping from a frame, while nearby what looks like an old-fashioned spin dryer is vibrating. Inside, three de-capped frames are being spun. Their honey – and some residual wax – is flung free and collects at the bottom. Josh will filter out the wax, and after a day Jill will drain the honey into jars.

Adam eventually agrees to 'Wednesday, barring accidents'.

'When you said Wednesday, I thought you meant first thing.' By first thing, David does not mean the sort of time Ruth starts milking, but later in the morning, because you cannot start combining until the dew has lifted from the crop.

'Sorry, David, we had a bit of trouble with the cutter bar. It'll take us a couple of hours to finish here and then we'll be right with you. Um . . .' Adam pauses.

'Yes?'

'Could you come over and be an escort, please? Mum and Brian have taken Ruairi out for the day, and everyone else is tied up.'

The combine is so wide that it nearly fills some of the lanes around Ambridge. For safety, one vehicle drives ahead and one behind, to warn unsuspecting motorists.

'Cheeky b—' Ending the phone call, David remembers that he is in the kitchen with his mother. 'Monkey' he ends, rather awkwardly.

Jill is removing a tray of flapjacks from the baking oven of the Aga. 'Don't mind me, David.'

You do not live your life on a farm without hearing some fruity language occasionally.

'That looks nice. Could I take . . .?'

'It needs to cool before I cut it. And these are for the fete, sorry.'

David knows better than to argue with his mother where flapjacks are concerned. Aside from their potential as projectiles, she once hit the roof after Pip helped herself to some without asking. But that was when Pip had first taken up with Toby, and Jill was still struggling with her visceral prejudice against all things Fairbrother. Pip knew they were reconciled a few months later, when Jill gave her some flapjacks to share.

'You could have one of those, if you like.' Jill nods at the muffin tin on the kitchen table.

'Brilliant.' David peels back the fluted paper and takes a big bite. His expression suddenly changes. 'Ugh . . . Oh, Mum, I'm sorry. Something's gone wrong with them.'

'I don't think so. Let me . . .' Jill breaks off a small piece and pops it in her mouth. 'You weren't expecting sweet, were you?'

'Well . . . yes.'

CHEESE, ONION AND BACON MUFFINS
Makes 12

225g self-raising flour
50g plain flour
1 tsp baking powder
½ tsp bicarbonate of soda
6 spring onions, trimmed and chopped
1 tsp butter
4 rashers of streaky bacon, diced
90ml rapeseed oil
150g plain yoghurt
125ml milk
1 egg, beaten
150g Cheddar cheese, grated
black pepper

Line a 12-hole muffin tin with paper cases. Preheat the oven to 200°C/Fan 180°C/Gas 6. Mix the flours, baking powder and bicarb in a bowl and add the chopped spring onions. Melt the butter in a small pan and fry the diced bacon until crisp and golden. Set aside to cool.

Mix the oil, yoghurt, milk and egg in a bowl and season with black pepper. Add the dry ingredients to the wet, then stir in 100g of the grated cheese and the cooled bacon. Mix as quickly and lightly as possible until just combined – don't over-mix or the muffins will be heavy. Spoon the mixture into the muffin cases, sprinkle with the remaining cheese and bake for 25 minutes. Remove and place the muffins on a wire rack to cool.

'Of course, once I knew what they were, they were delicious!'

It is David's turn on moisture meter duties. On her way to bring the cows in for milking, Pip wanted to see how he is. He confesses to being a lot happier now that Adam is getting on with it.

Once their grain is safely harvested, David or Josh will bale the straw and transport it to the barn, ready for winter bedding and feed. Pity the local driver who, having had last week's journey delayed by the slow progress of the combine, now ends up crawling behind Brookfield's tractor, the trailer heaped unfeasibly high with bales. Soon afterwards (David hopes), Adam will prepare their fields for sowing the next crop.

'Them bruschetta look nice.'

'Actually, they're bruschetta, Jolene.'

'That's what I said.'

'No, you said "broo-shetta". It's actually pronounced "broo-sketta".'

Jim feels that no situation is too informal for some linguistic pedantry, and the Ambridge Tearoom tent at the

Summer Fete is no exception. He raises his voice over the drums and shakers of the samba band parading outside. Despite their tropical garb, the typical member of 'Espírito de Paixão' is a semi-retired geography teacher from Waterley Cross.

'Oliver! Can you help me out? What is this, please?'

Oliver ambles over and surveys the cakes and savouries. 'You mean the bruschetta?'

Jim is vindicated, but Jolene is unconcerned. 'Actually, I've changed my mind. I'll have a couple of paninis.'

The two men exchange glances. While Fallon serves her mother, they start to explain, without much success, that 'panini' is already plural, so 'paninis' is a crime against language.

BRUSCHETTA
Makes 4

4 slices of sourdough
  bread
2 tbsp olive oil

Tomato topping
4 ripe tomatoes
2 tbsp olive oil
1 tbsp balsamic vinegar
1 garlic clove, halved
handful of basil leaves
salt and black pepper

Pea and ricotta topping
200g frozen peas
100g ricotta
1 tsp finely chopped mint,
  plus extra to garnish
salt and black pepper

*Goats' cheese and sun-
  dried tomato topping*
150g goats' cheese log
2 tbsp crème fraiche
1 tsp chopped parsley
1 tsp chopped thyme
4 sun-dried tomatoes, cut
  into strips
salt and black pepper

Heat a ridged griddle pan. Brush both sides of the bread with oil, then toast on the griddle until lightly browned. Prepare your topping – each recipe makes enough for 4 slices of bread.

For the tomato topping, dice the tomatoes, dress them with the olive oil and vinegar and season with salt and black pepper. Rub the bread with a cut clove of garlic, then pile on the tomatoes. Add a few basil leaves and serve at once.

For the pea and ricotta topping, put the peas in a bowl and add boiling water. Drain and refresh under cold water. Put the peas in a food processor and add the ricotta, chopped mint and seasoning, then blitz to a purée. Spread this mixture on the toasted sourdough and garnish with more chopped mint.

For the goats' cheese topping, mix the cheese and crème fraiche with the chopped herbs. Preheat the grill. Spread the mixture on the toasted sourdough and top with a few strips of sun-dried tomato. Grill until the cheese has melted, then season with salt and black pepper.

'That was rubbish, Dad! You didn't hit one!'

'I wasn't ready.' Shamefaced Roy hands the Splat the Rat truncheon back to Richard Thwaite.

'Give me that,' says Phoebe. 'And let me show you how it's done.'

While Emma draws her ticket at the bottle stall next door, Josh and Ed are talking sheep.

'Are you putting the ram in with yours already?' Josh asks. He has been helping David select Brookfield's poorest-quality ewes for culling, but tupping is a while away yet.

'Yeah, and AI'ing some. I need to lamb in January so they're as big as possible for the show season.'

'Oh, of course.'

Emma unfolds the slip of paper. 'Three six eight.'

Jennifer locates Emma's prize. 'A jar of lemon curd!'

'Really . . .?' She was hoping for the prosecco.

Jennifer bristles. 'It's very nice. I made it myself.'

'Oh . . . yeah, I'm sure it'll be lovely. Thank you very much.'

LEMON CURD
Makes a couple of jars

3 unwaxed lemons
120g butter, cut into cubes
225g granulated sugar
3 eggs, beaten

Wash and dry the lemons. Zest them, then cut them in half and squeeze out the juice.

Place a bowl over a pan of simmering water – the bottom of the bowl shouldn't touch the water. Add the butter and once it has melted, stir in the sugar, lemon zest and juice. Add the eggs and stir over a gentle heat until the mixture thickens and coats the back of a wooden spoon.

Pour into sterilised jars and cover. Leave to cool, then store in the fridge. It keeps for a week or so. Perfect on scones or for sandwiching a Victoria sponge.

An almighty splash and a roar of laughter announces that Rex's powerful throw has hit the target at the Dunk the Vicar stand. Alan rises from the paddling pool, spluttering.

The atmosphere by the WI tent is rather less riotous. Brian is seated at an outdoor table, enjoying a savoury flan with salad. The courgettes have come from Bridge Farm, the last of this year's crop.

ROASTED COURGETTE TART
Serves 4–6

Filling
2 onions, peeled and thickly sliced
3 courgettes, sliced diagonally
3 tbsp olive oil
3 thyme sprigs
3 eggs, beaten
250ml crème fraiche
150ml double cream
75g Parmesan cheese, grated
salt and black pepper

Shortcrust pastry
250g plain flour, plus extra for rolling
½ tsp salt
150g cold butter, diced
1 egg, beaten

AUGUST

Preheat the oven to 220°C/Fan 200°C/Gas 7. Put the sliced
onions and courgettes into a baking tray and drizzle over
the olive oil. Mix to coat all the vegetables in the oil. Add the
thyme sprigs and season with salt and pepper, then roast for
20 minutes.

Meanwhile make the pastry. Put the flour and salt in a food
processor and add the butter, then pulse until the mixture
resembles breadcrumbs. Keep the motor running and add
the beaten egg and process until the mixture starts to come
together. Remove the pastry from the processor and roll it out
on a floured surface. Line a 25cm flan tin with the pastry and
lightly prick it all over with a fork. Place it in the fridge to chill
for 30 minutes.

Preheat the oven to 190°C/Fan 170°C/Gas 5. Cover the pastry
with baking paper and fill with baking beans, then bake it
blind for 15 minutes or until just set. Remove the beans and
parchment and put the pastry back in the oven for another
5 minutes. Turn the oven down to 180°C/Fan 160°C/Gas 4.

Fill the pastry case with the roasted vegetables. Mix the
eggs with crème fraiche, double cream and Parmesan and
season with salt and pepper. Carefully pour this mixture over
the vegetables, then bake the tart in the oven for about 30
minutes. Good hot or cold.

Toby wanders by, chewing a flapjack. 'Oh . . . Brian . . .' Toby swallows his mouthful. 'Is Adam about? I've got a brilliant business idea he might be interested in.'

Brian's expression betrays his opinion of Toby's business acumen.

'No, he couldn't make it. He's got work to do.'

A mile from the village green, a tractor and seed drill track their steady back-and-forth over the soil. And so the farming wheel continues to turn . . .

ACKNOWLEDGEMENTS

As with any book, the author's name on the jacket is just the visible tip of an iceberg (lettuce?) of contributors. I am very grateful to all these people, and more:

Catherine Phipps and Jinny Johnson for their food knowledge and experience, wise counsel and booky know-how.

Emanuel Santos for the illustrations on the opening pages for each chapter.

At Orion:
Amanda Harris, Jennifer Kerslake, Helen Ewing, Katie Horrocks, Kate Moreton, Amy Davies and Shyam Kumar.

At the BBC:
Archers editor Jeremy Howe, who trusted me with the project, and especially for his thoughts on narrative.

Archers agricultural advisor Sarah Swadling, for farming wisdom and good humour.

Hannah Ratcliffe and Jessica Bunch, who helped in the initial brainstorming, for comments on the text and being general good eggs.

Mel Ward for checking the text against *The Archers* voluminous archive.

ACKNOWLEDGEMENTS

Ellie Caddell at BBC Business Affairs, and Sean Harwood in publicity.

And to all my colleagues past and present on *The Archers*' production, writing, acting and technical teams, who have kept this extraordinary programme on the air since 1951.

Special gratitude to Fiona Campbell, for unstinting support at a time of considerable pressure, and for reading several iterations of the manuscript.

Finally – and most importantly – to the millions of listeners, without whom all this work would be completely pointless. For over a quarter of a century in a range of jobs I could not have dreamed of as a young *Archers* fan, I thank you.

INDEX OF RECIPES